FIRST 50 HYMNS

YOU SHOULD PLAY ON THE PIANO

ISBN 978-1-5400-2602-6

Visit Hal Leonard Online at
www.halleonard.com

Contact Us:
Hal Leonard
7777 West Bluemound Road
Milwaukee, WI 53213
Email: info@halleonard.com

In Europe contact:
Hal Leonard Europe Limited
Distribution Centre, Newmarket Road
Bury St Edmunds, Suffolk, IP33 3YB
Email: info@halleonardeurope.com

In Australia contact:
Hal Leonard Australia Pty. Ltd.
4 Lentara Court
Cheltenham, Victoria, 3192 Australia
Email: info@halleonard.com.au

ABIDE WITH ME

Words by HENRY F. LYTE
Music by WILLIAM H. MONK

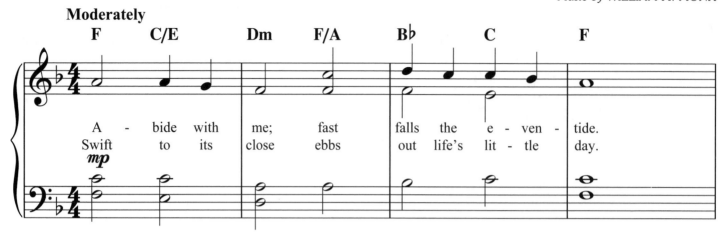

A - bide with me; fast falls the e - ven - tide.
Swift to its close ebbs out life's lit - tle day.

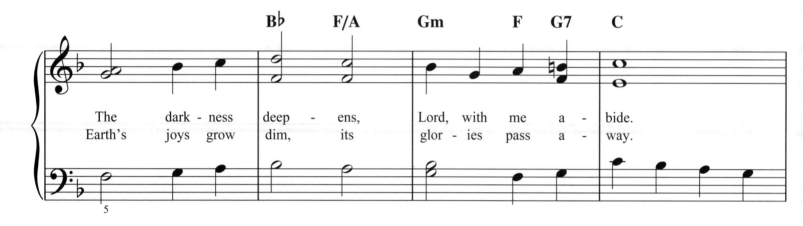

The dark - ness deep - ens, Lord, with me a - bide.
Earth's joys grow dim, its glor - ies pass a - way.

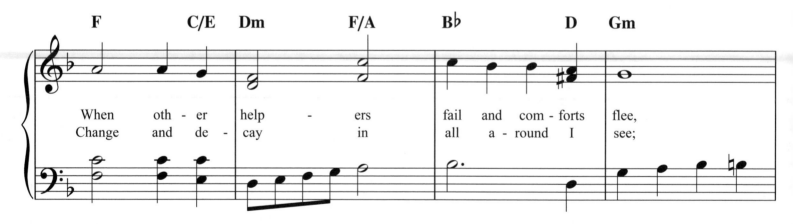

When oth - er help - ers fail and com - forts flee,
Change and de - cay in all a - round I see;

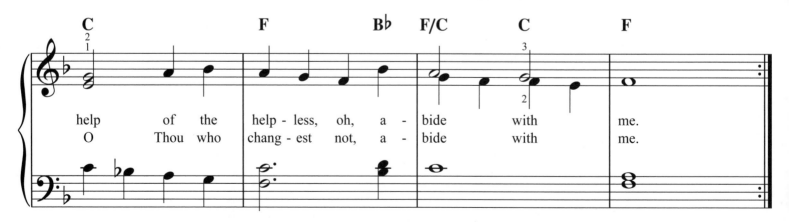

help of the help - less, oh, a - bide with me.
O Thou who chang - est not, a - bide with me.

AMAZING GRACE

Words by JOHN NEWTON
From *A Collection of Sacred Ballads*
Traditional American Melody
From Carrell and Clayton's *Virginia Harmony*

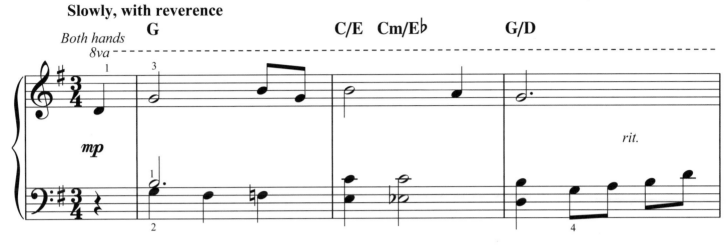

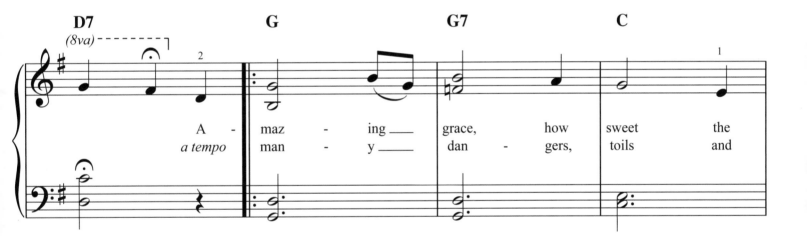

A- maz - ing ___ grace, how sweet the

man - y ___ dan - gers, toils and

sound that saved a ___ wretch like me! ___

snares I have al - read - y come. ___

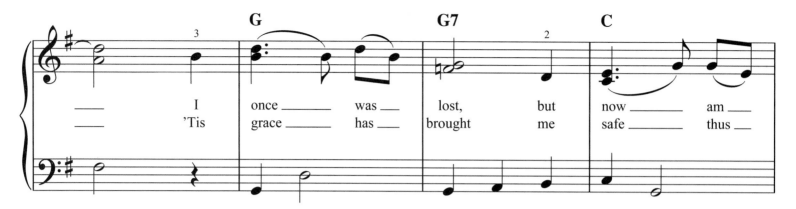

I   once _____ was _____ lost,   but   now _____ am _____
'Tis   grace _____ has _____ brought   me   safe _____ thus _____

found,   was   blind,   but ____   now   I   see. _____
far,   and   grace   will ____   lead   me   home. _____

_____   'Twas   grace   that ____   taught   my   heart   to
_____   The   Lord   has ____   prom -   ised   good   to

fear   and   grace   my _____   fears   re -
me,   His   word   my _____   hope   se -

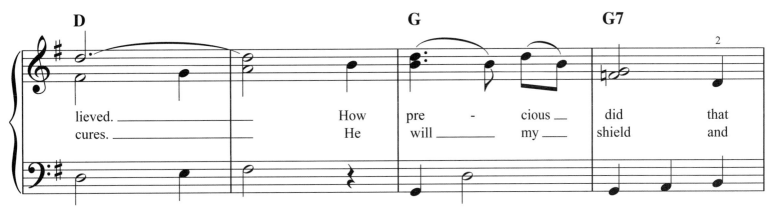

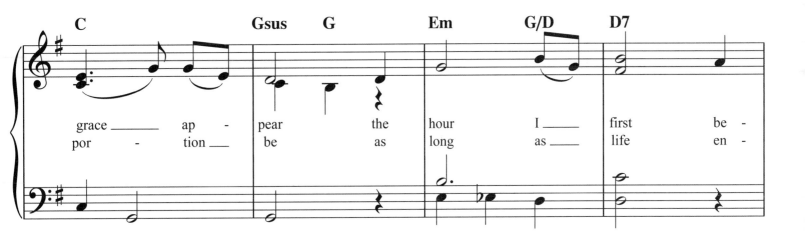

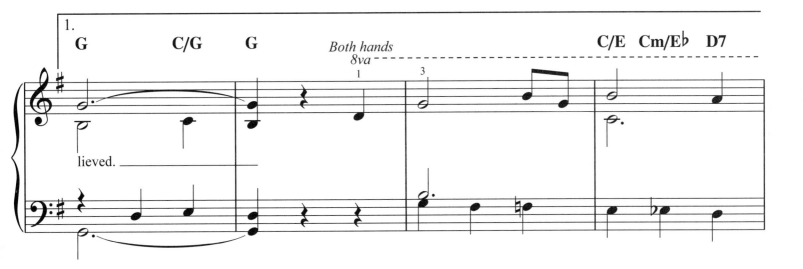

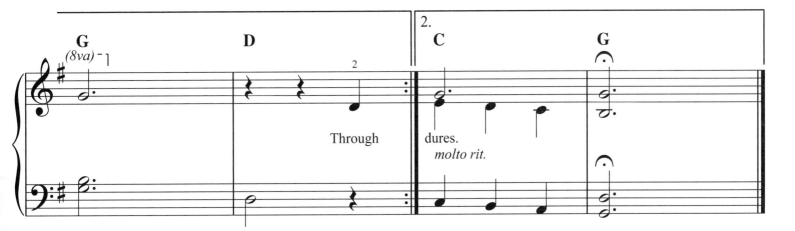

ALL CREATURES OF OUR GOD AND KING

Words by FRANCIS OF ASSISI
Translated by WILLIAM HENRY DRAPER
Music from *Geistliche Kirchengesang*

Stately

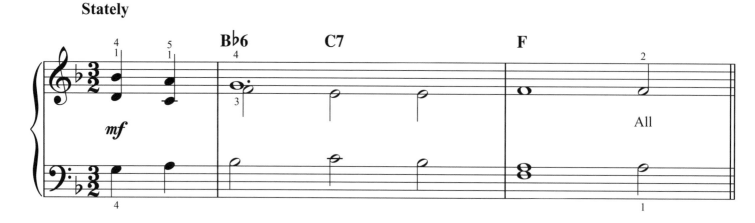

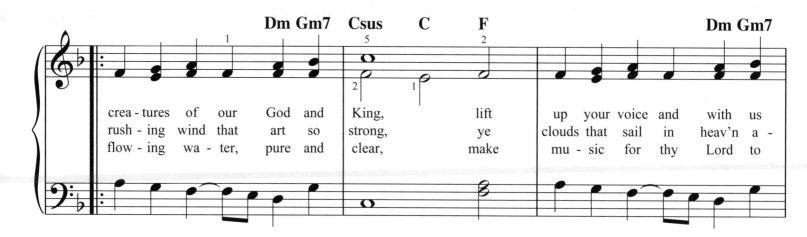

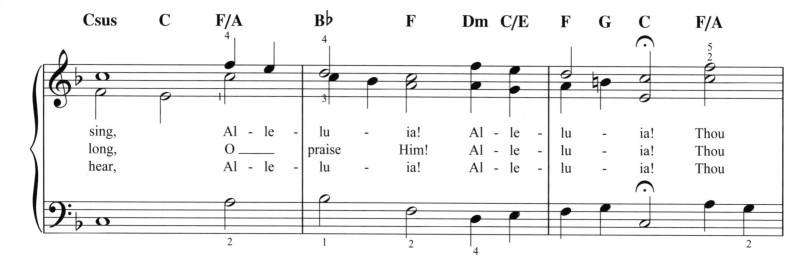

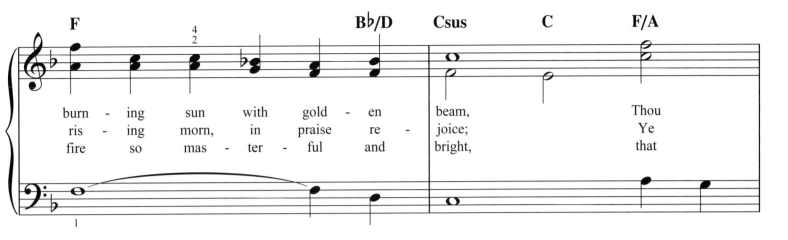

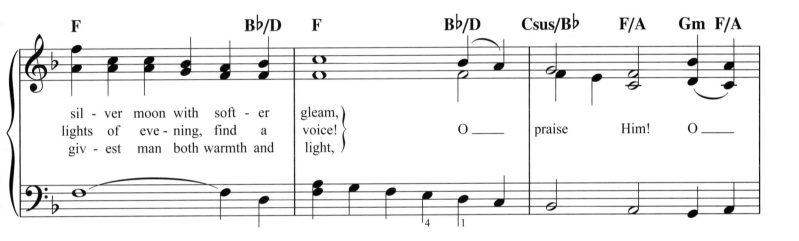

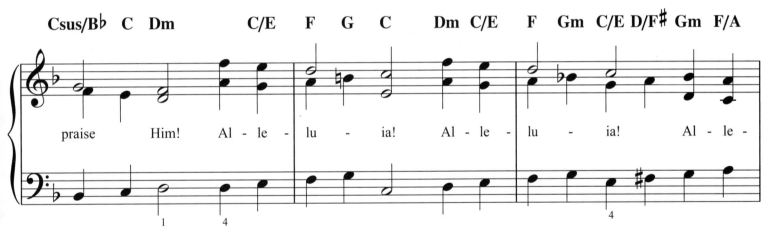

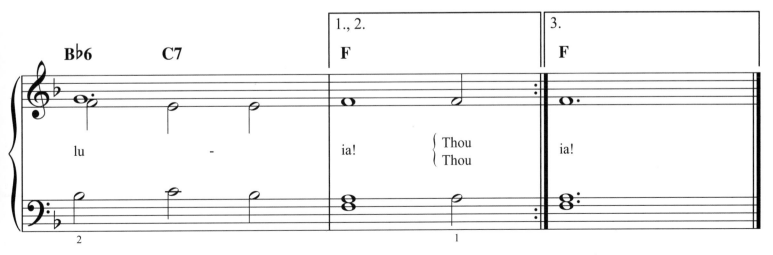

ALL HAIL THE POWER
OF JESUS' NAME

Words by EDWARD PERRONET
Altered by JOHN RIPPON
Music by OLIVER HOLDEN

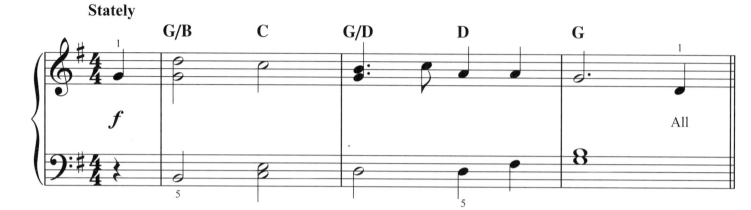

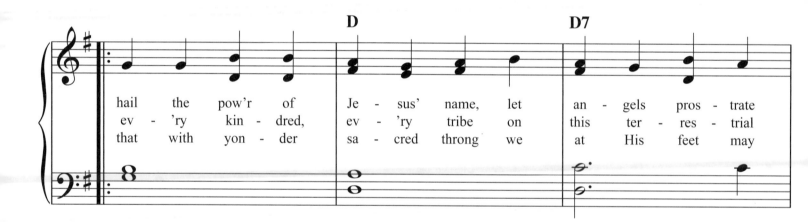

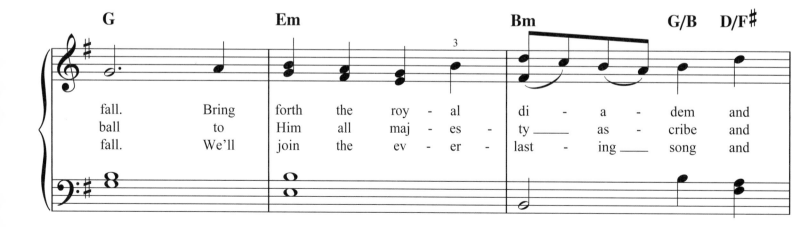

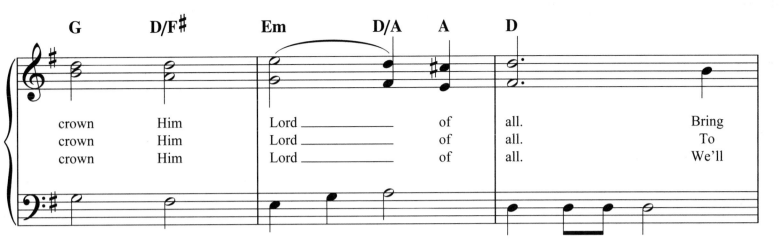

crown Him   Lord _____ of   all.   Bring
crown Him   Lord _____ of   all.   To
crown Him   Lord _____ of   all.   We'll

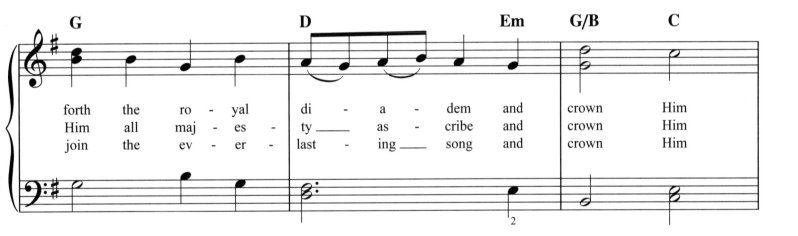

forth the ro - yal   di - a - dem and   crown Him
Him all maj - es - ty _____ as - cribe and   crown Him
join the ev - er - last - ing _____ song and   crown Him

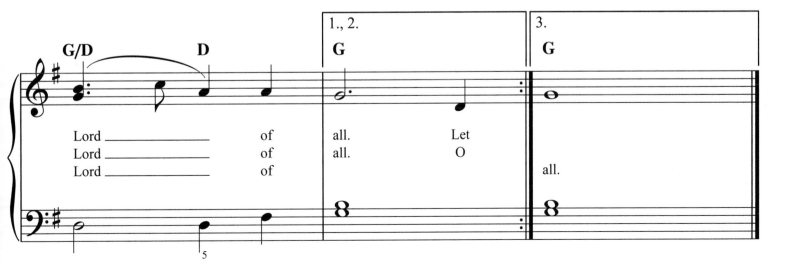

Lord _____ of all.   Let
Lord _____ of all.   O
Lord _____ of   all.

AMERICA, THE BEAUTIFUL

Words by KATHARINE LEE BATES
Music by SAMUEL A. WARD

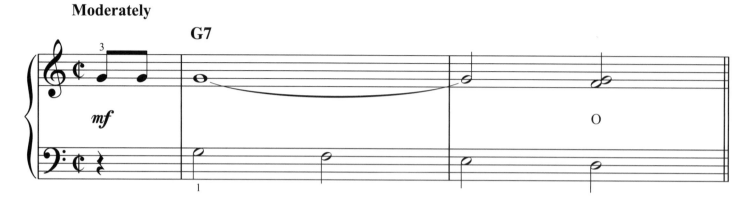

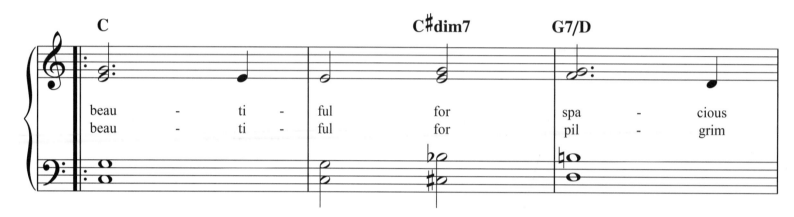

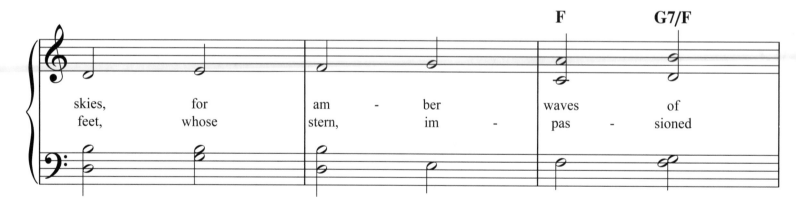

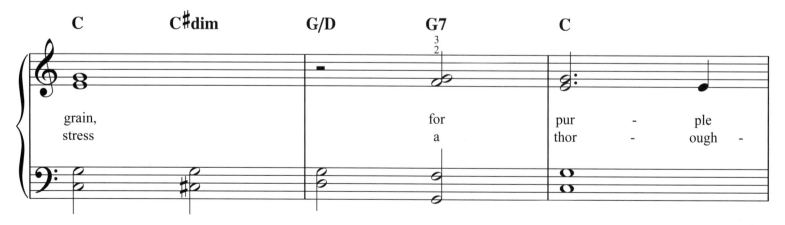

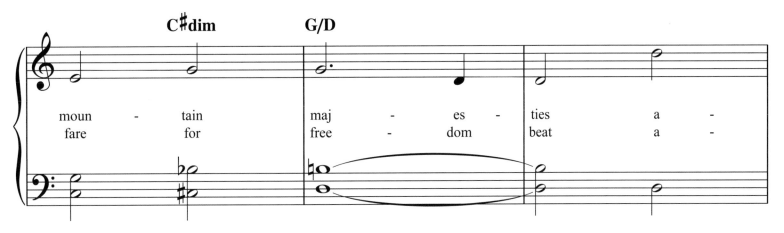

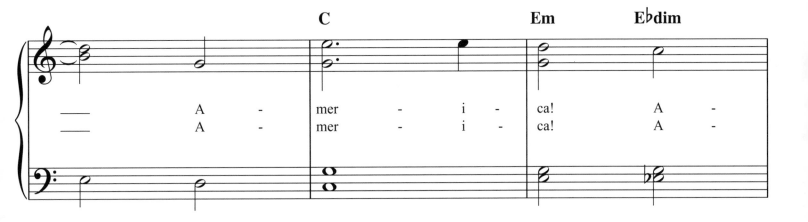

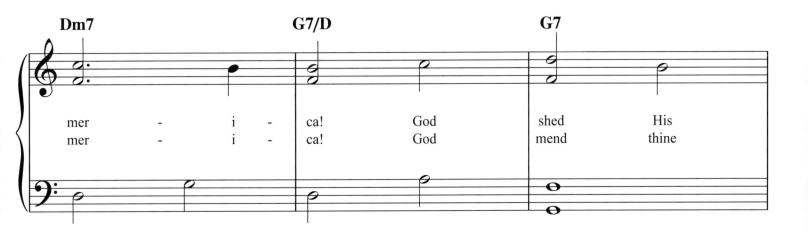

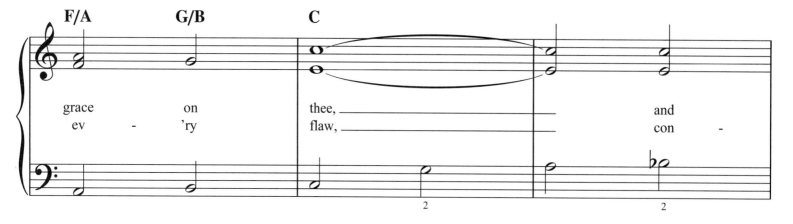

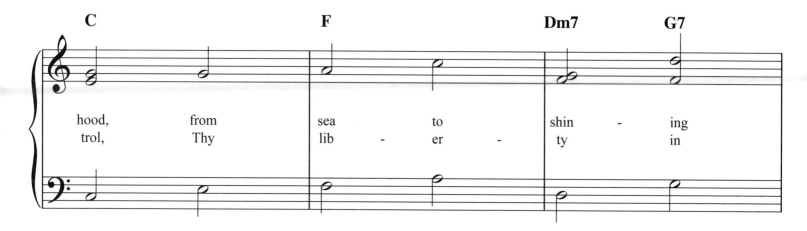

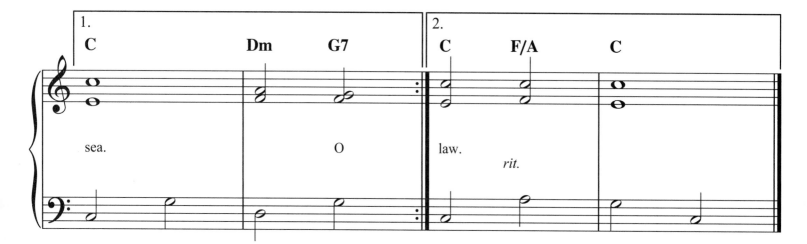

BATTLE HYMN OF THE REPUBLIC

Words by JULIA WARD HOWE
Music by WILLIAM STEFFE

Moderately slow, in 2

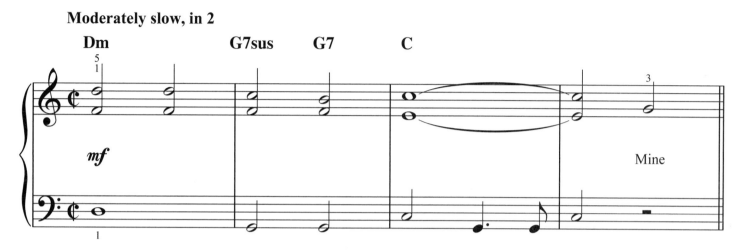

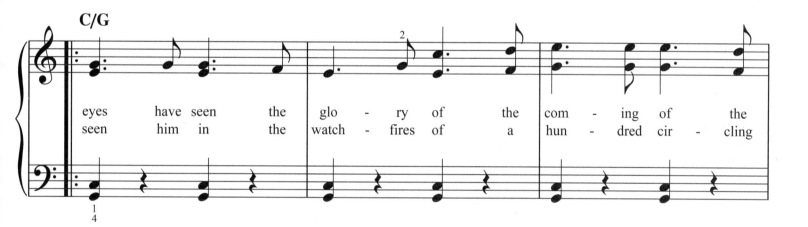

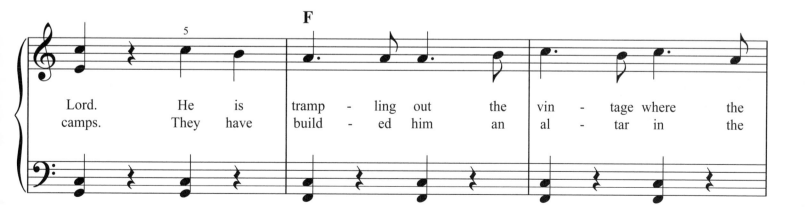

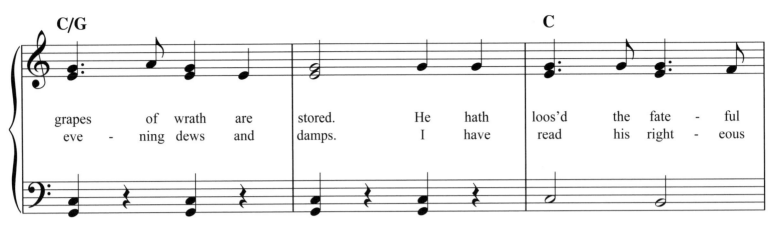

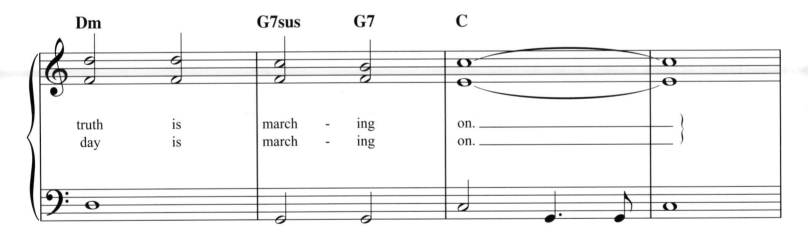

jah! Glo - ry, glo - ry, hal - le -

lu - jah! Glo - ry, glo - ry, hal - le -

lu - jah! His truth is march - ing

on. I have on.

BE THOU MY VISION

Traditional Irish
Translated by MARY E. BYRNE

COME, CHRISTIANS, JOIN TO SING

Words by CHRISTIAN HENRY BATEMAN
Traditional Spanish Melody

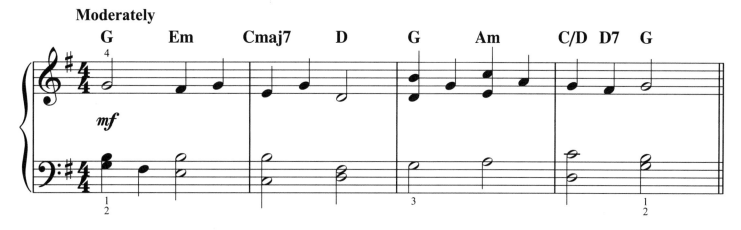

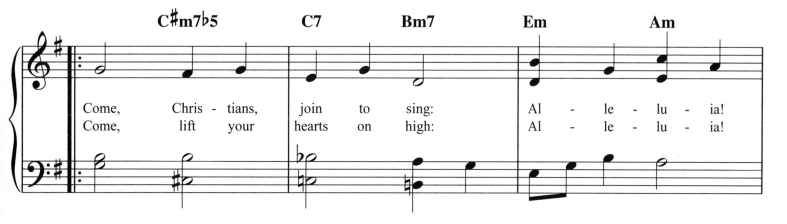

Come, Chris - tians, join to sing: Al - le - lu - ia!
Come, lift your hearts on high: Al - le - lu - ia!

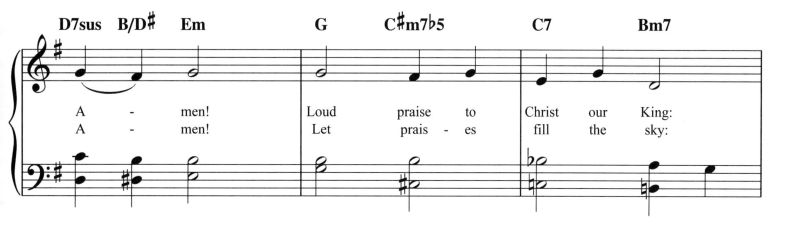

A - men! Loud praise to Christ our King:
A - men! Let prais - es fill the sky:

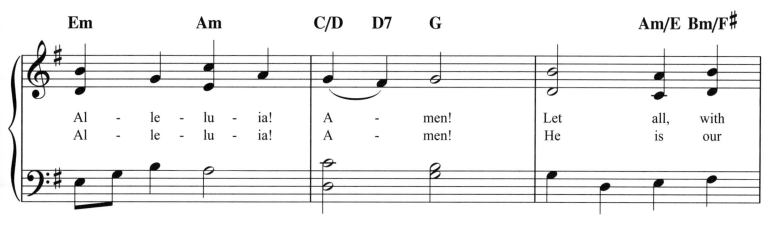

Al - le - lu - ia! A - men! Let all, with
Al - le - lu - ia! A - men! He is our

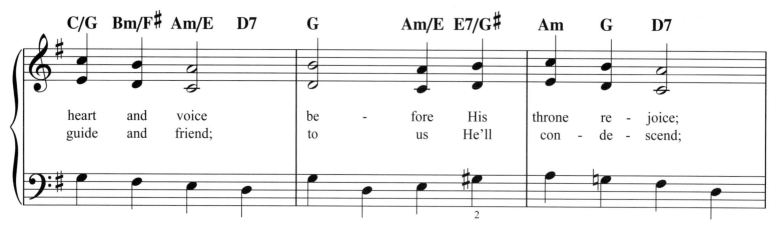

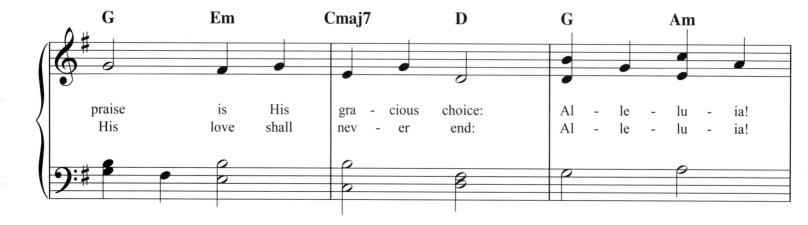

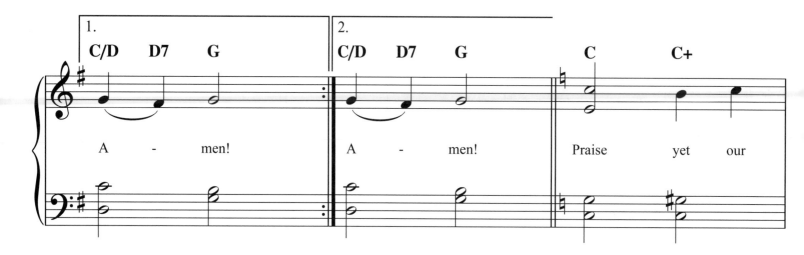

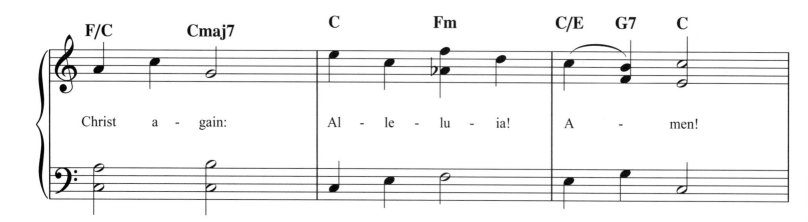

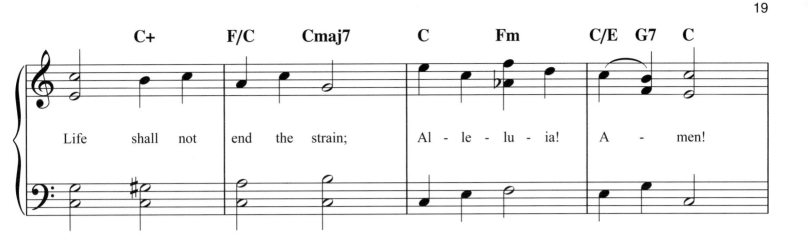

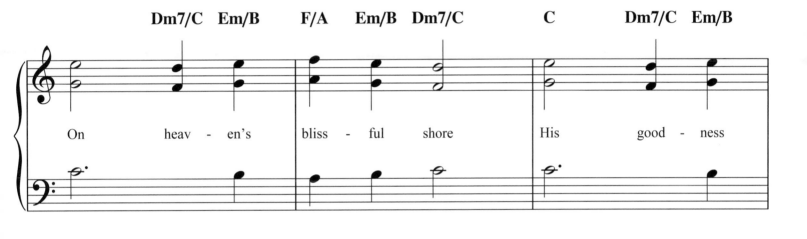

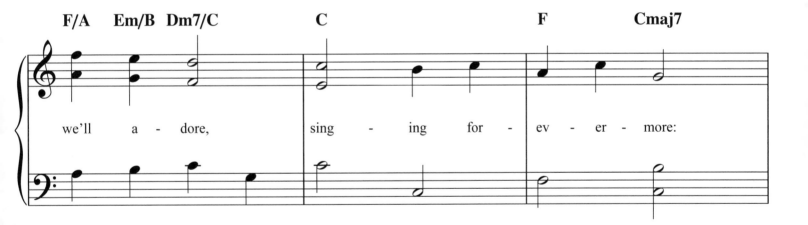

BEAUTIFUL SAVIOR

Words from *Munsterisch Gesangbuch*
Translated by JOSEPH A. SEISS
Music adapted from Silesian Folk Tune

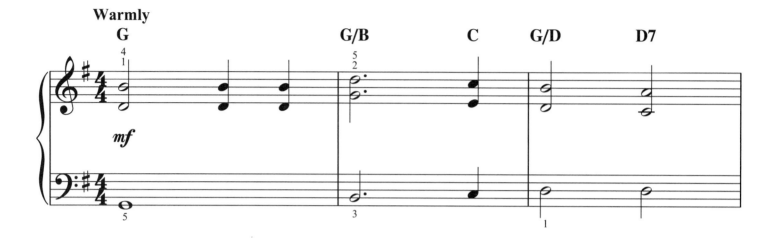

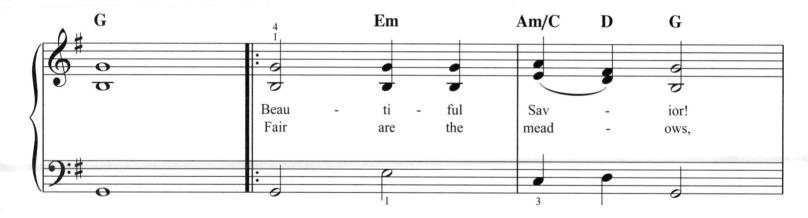

Beau - ti - ful Sav - ior!
Fair are the mead - ows,

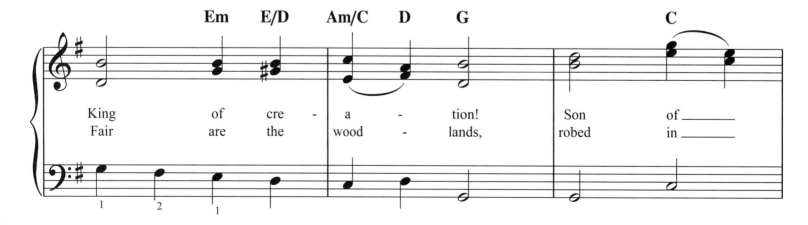

King of cre - a - tion! Son of _____
Fair are the wood - lands, robed in _____

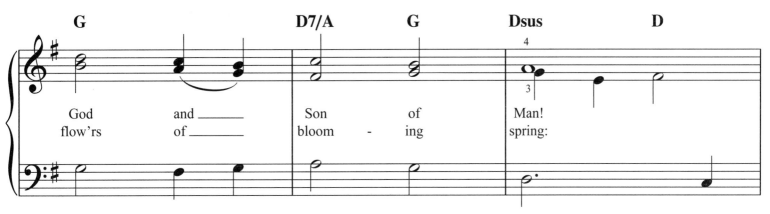

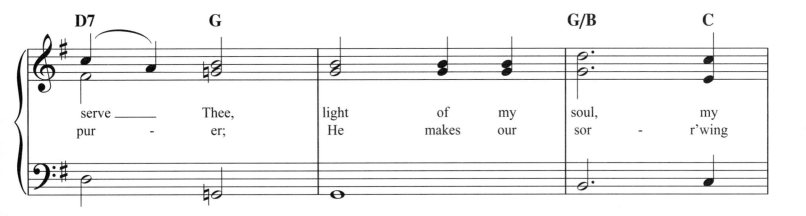

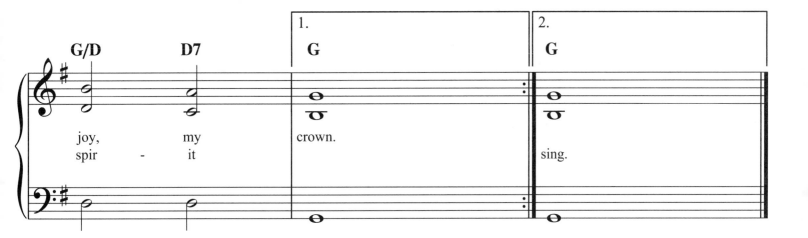

BLESSED ASSURANCE

Lyrics by FANNY J. CROSBY
Music by PHOEBE PALMER KNAPP

With movement

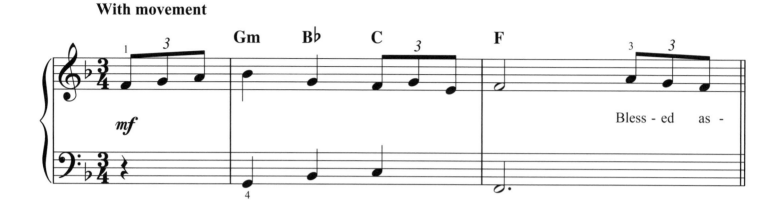

Bless - ed as -

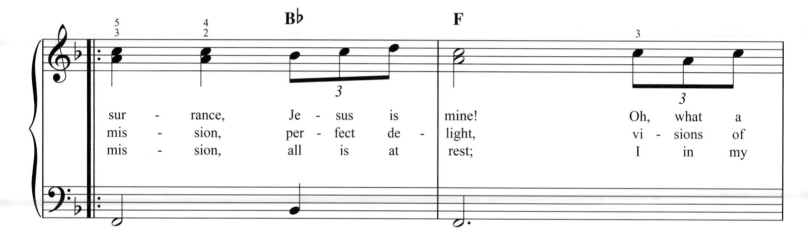

sur - rance,   Je - sus is   mine!   Oh, what a
mis - sion,   per - fect de - light,   vi - sions of
mis - sion,   all is at   rest;   I in my

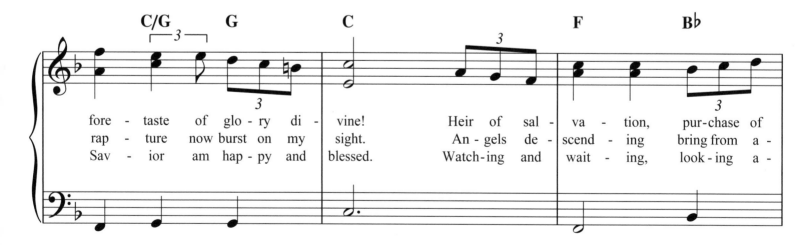

fore - taste of glo - ry di - vine!   Heir of sal - va - tion,   pur-chase of
rap - ture now burst on my   sight.   An - gels de - scend - ing   bring from a -
Sav - ior am hap - py and   blessed.   Watch-ing and wait - ing,   look - ing a -

God, born of His Spir - it, washed in His blood.
bove ech - oes of mer - cy, whis - pers of love.
bove, filled with His good - ness, lost in His love. This is my

sto - ry, this is my song, prais - ing my Sav - ior all the day

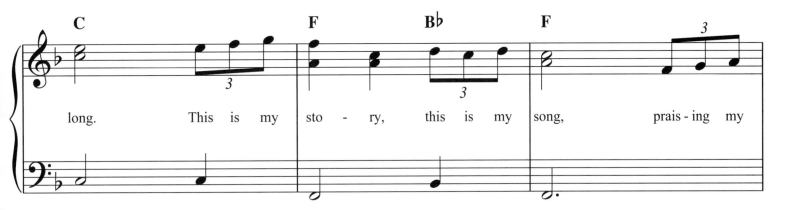

long. This is my sto - ry, this is my song, prais - ing my

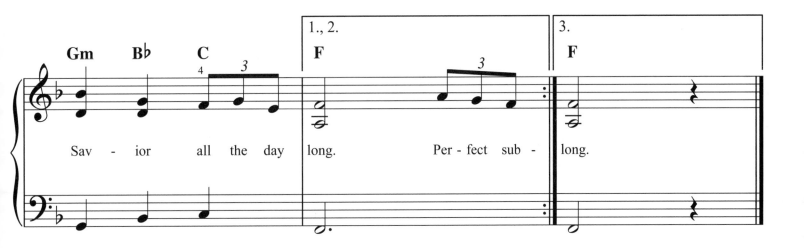

Sav - ior all the day long. Per - fect sub - long.

COME, THOU ALMIGHTY KING

Traditional
Music by FELICE DE GIARDINI

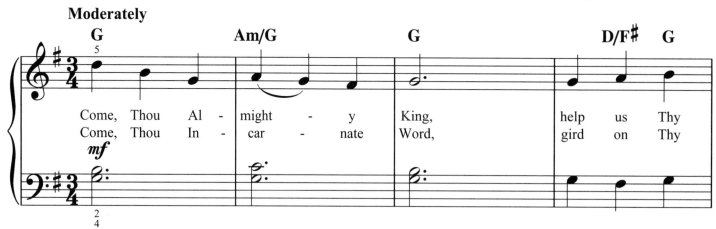

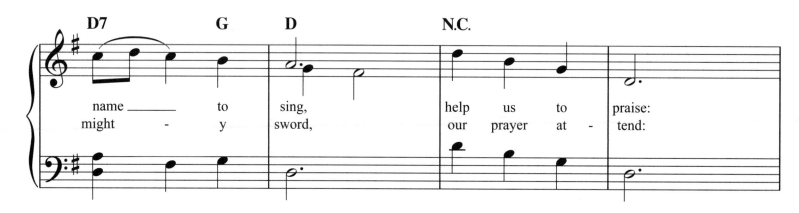

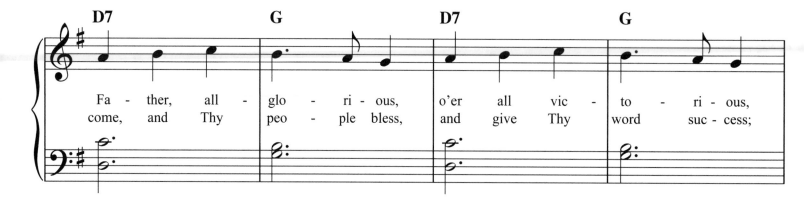

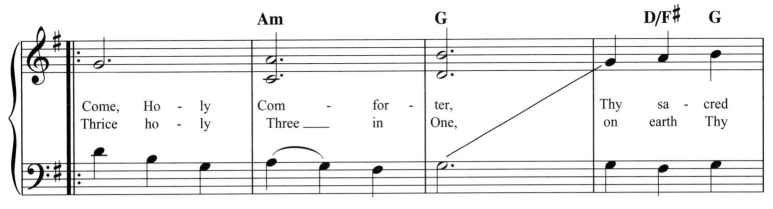
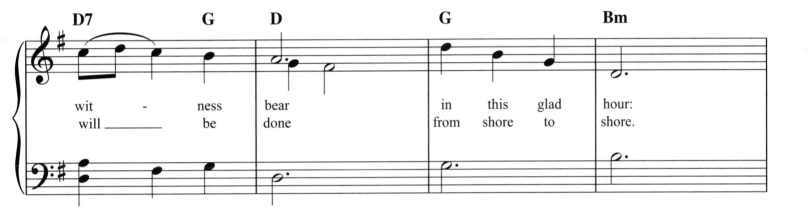
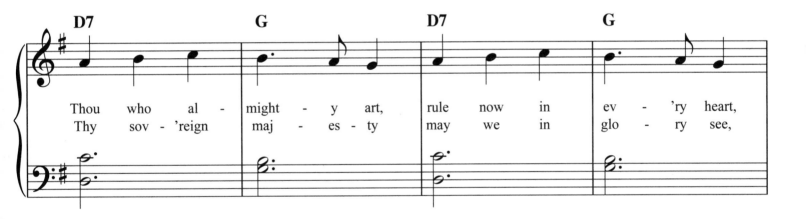
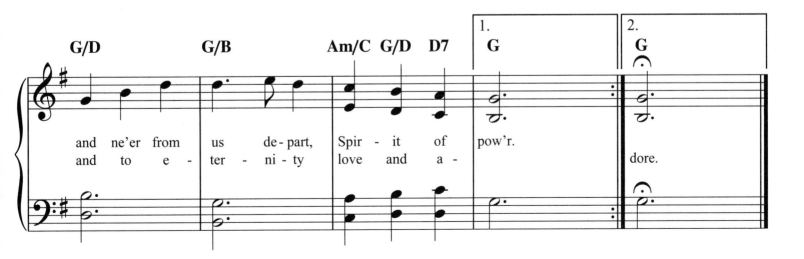

COME, THOU FOUNT OF EVERY BLESSING

Words by ROBERT ROBINSON
Music from JOHN WYETH's *Repository of Sacred Music*

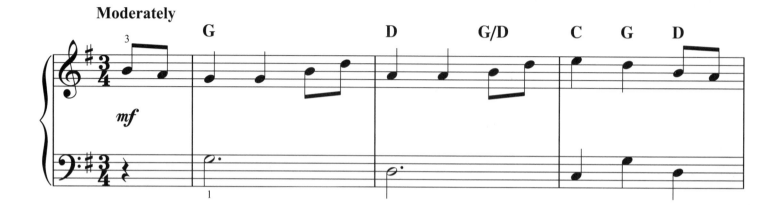

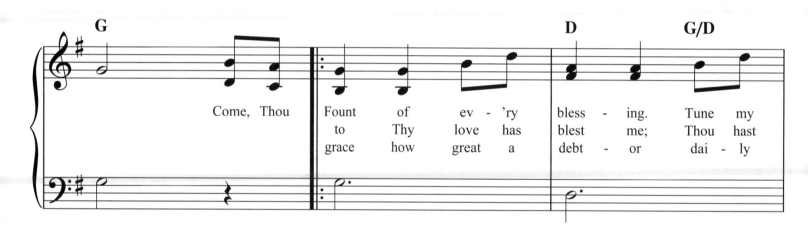

Come, Thou | Fount of ev-'ry bless-ing. Tune my
| to Thy love has blest me; Thou hast
| grace how great a debt-or dai-ly

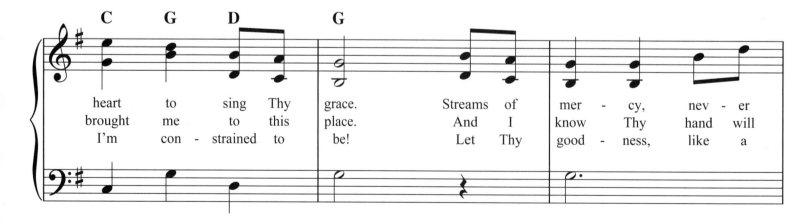

heart to sing Thy | grace. | Streams of | mer-cy, nev-er
brought me to this place. | And I know Thy hand will
I'm con-strained to be! | Let Thy good-ness, like a

27

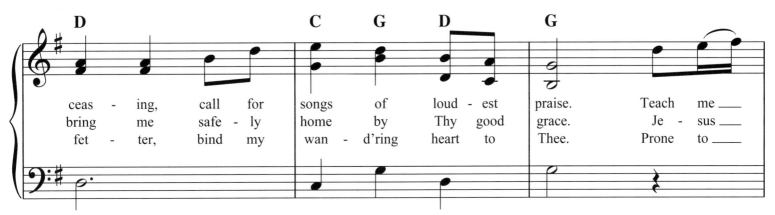

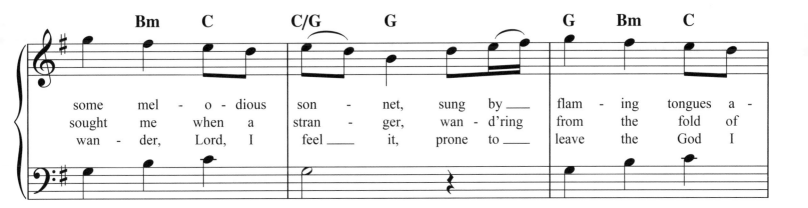

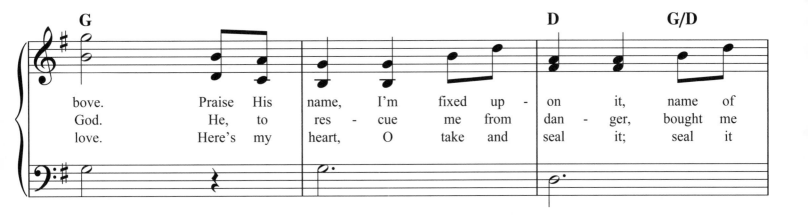

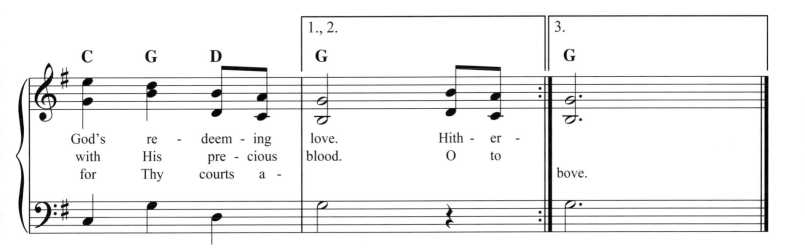

COME, YE THANKFUL PEOPLE, COME

Words by HENRY ALFORD
Music by GEORGE JOB ELVEY

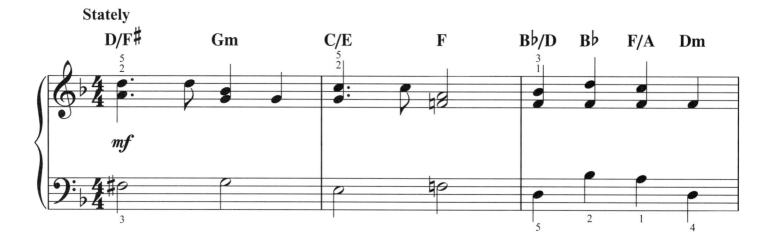

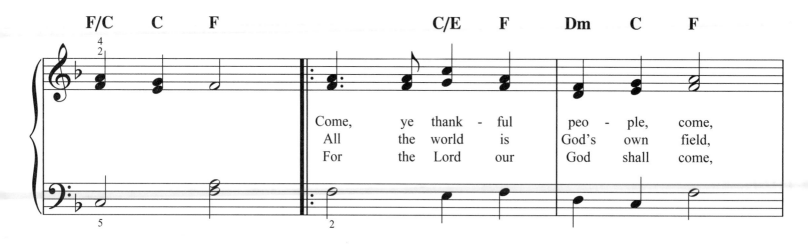

Come, ye thank - ful peo - ple, come,
All the world is God's own field,
For the Lord our God shall come,

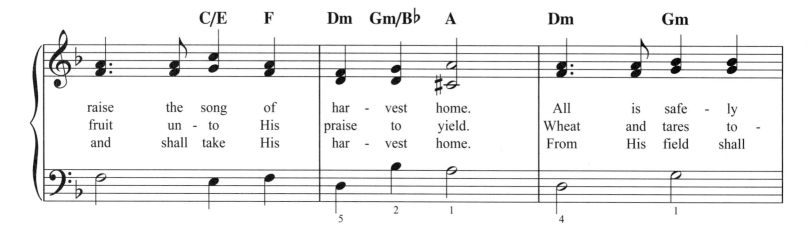

raise the song of har - vest home. All is safe - ly
fruit un - to His praise to yield. Wheat and tares to-
and shall take His har - vest home. From His field shall

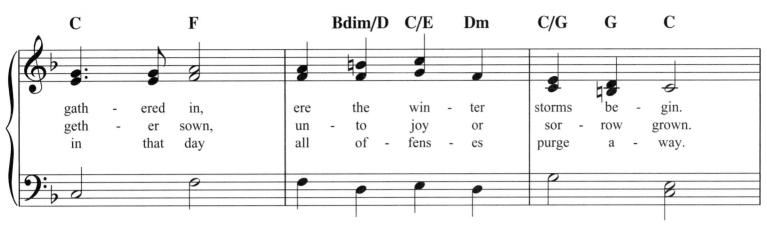

gath - ered in,　ere　the　win - ter　storms　be - gin.
geth - er sown,　un - to　joy　or　sor - row　grown.
in　that　day　all　of - fens - es　purge　a - way.

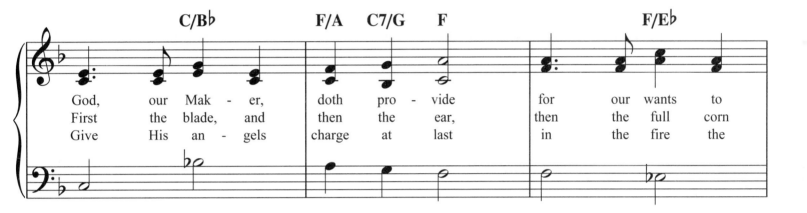

God,　our　Mak - er,　doth　pro - vide　for　our　wants　to
First　the　blade,　and　then　the　ear,　then　the　full　corn
Give　His　an - gels　charge　at　last　in　the　fire　the

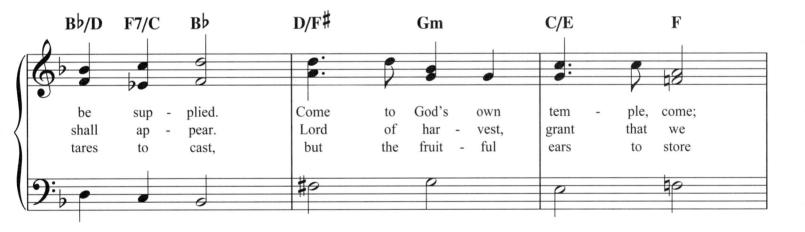

be　sup - plied.　Come　to　God's　own　tem - ple,　come;
shall　ap - pear.　Lord　of　har - vest,　grant　that　we
tares　to　cast,　but　the　fruit - ful　ears　to　store

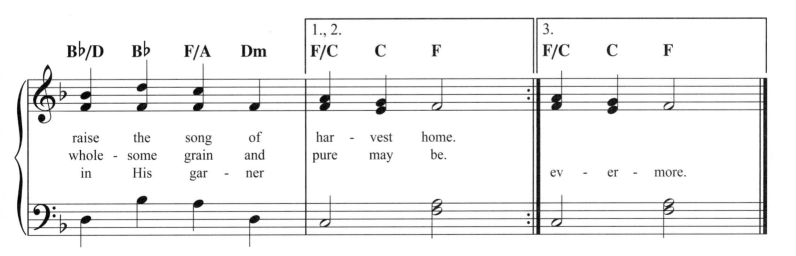

raise　the　song　of　har - vest　home.
whole - some　grain　and　pure　may　be.
in　His　gar - ner

ev - er - more.

CROWN HIM WITH MANY CROWNS

Words by MATTHEW BRIDGES
and GODFREY THRING
Music by GEORGE JOB ELVEY

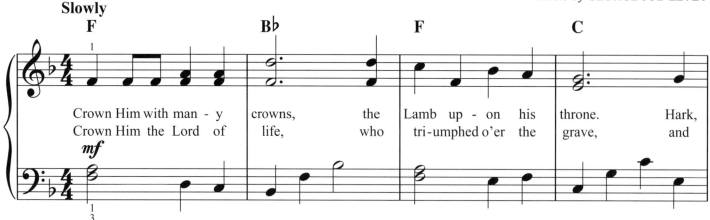

Crown Him with man - y crowns, the Lamb up - on his throne. Hark,
Crown Him the Lord of life, who tri - umphed o'er the grave, and

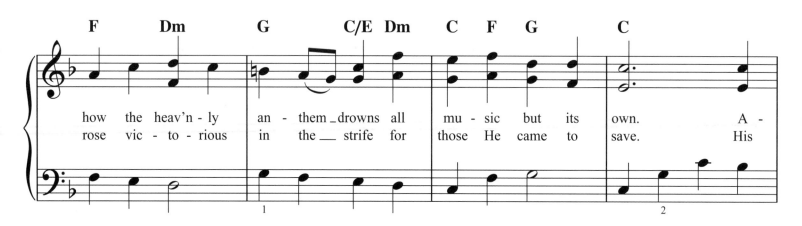

how the heav'n - ly an - them drowns all mu - sic but its own. A -
rose vic - to - rious in the strife for those He came to save. His

wake, my soul, and sing of Him who died for thee, and
glo - ries now we sing, who died, and rose on high, who

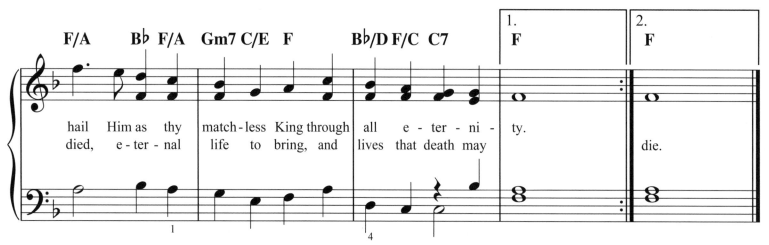

hail Him as thy match - less King through all e - ter - ni - ty.
died, e - ter - nal life to bring, and lives that death may die.

FOR THE BEAUTY OF THE EARTH

Words by FOLLIOT S. PIERPOINT
Music by CONRAD KOCHER

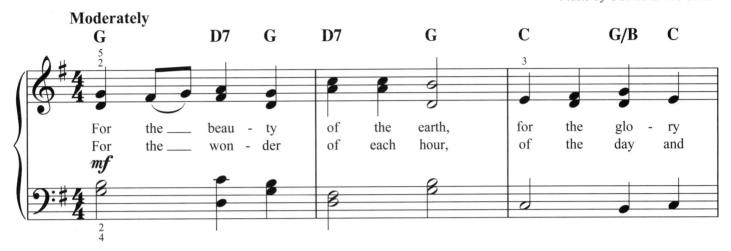

For the ___ beau - ty of the earth, for the glo - ry
For the ___ won - der of each hour, of the day and

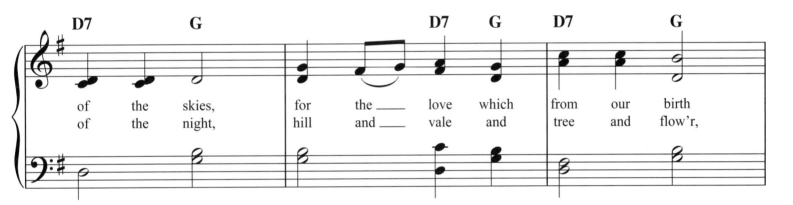

of the skies, for the ___ love which from our birth
of the night, hill and ___ vale which and tree and flow'r,

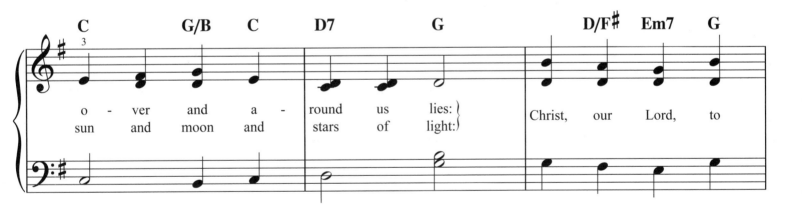

o - ver and a - round us lies: } Christ, our Lord, to
sun and moon and stars of light: }

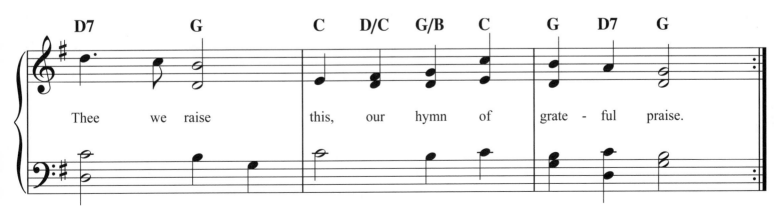

Thee we raise this, our hymn of grate - ful praise.

ETERNAL FATHER, STRONG TO SAVE

Words by WILLIAM WHITING
Music by JOHN BACCHUS DYKES

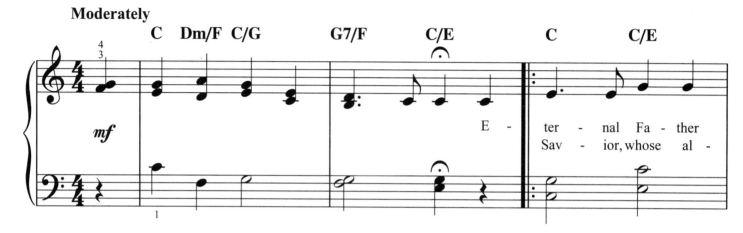

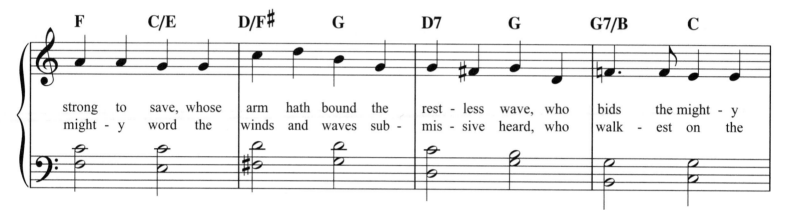

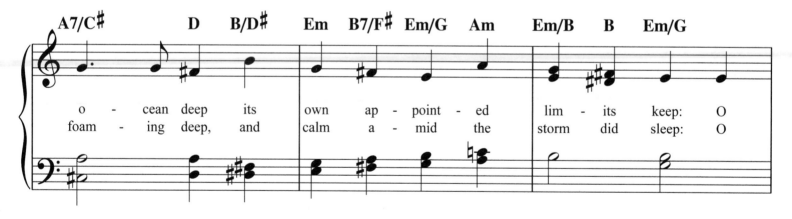

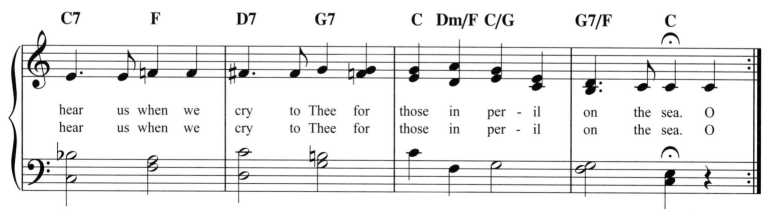

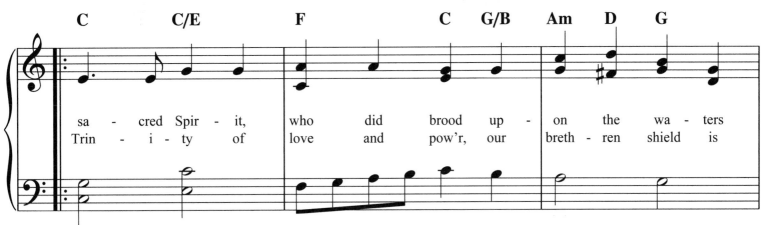

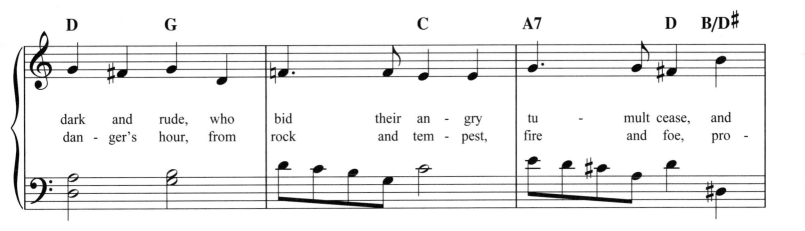

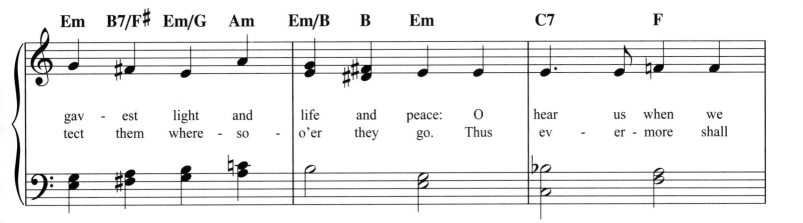

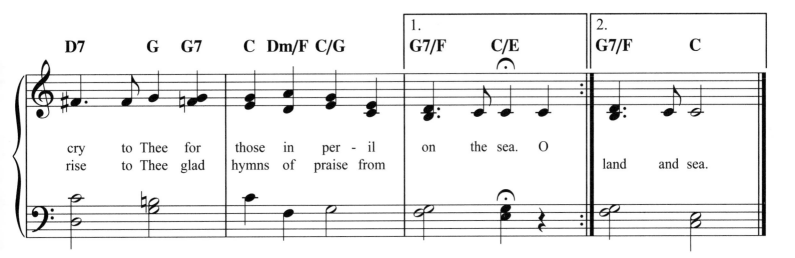

HAVE THINE OWN WAY, LORD

Words by ADELAIDE A. POLLARD
Music by GEORGE C. STEBBINS

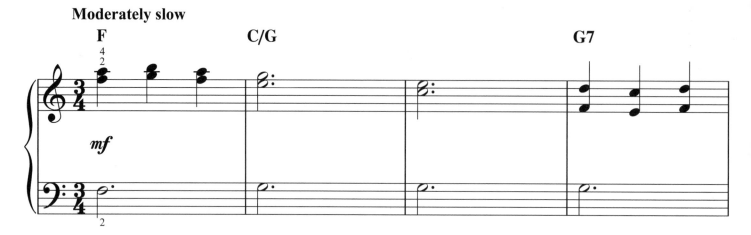

Have Thine own way,
Have Thine own way,

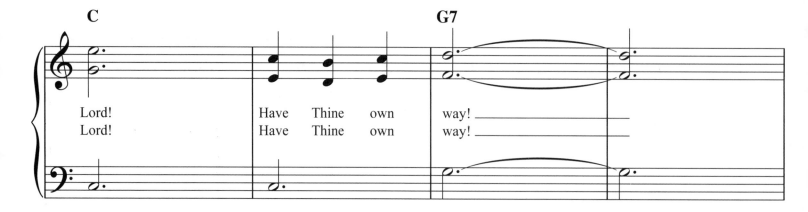

Lord!   Have Thine own way! _____
Lord!   Have Thine own way! _____

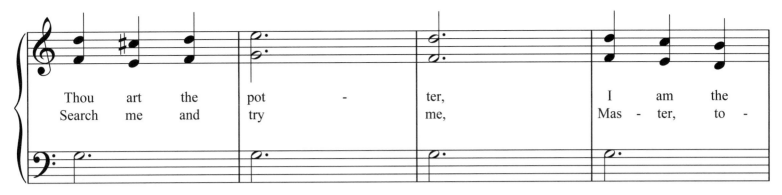

Thou art the pot - ter, I am the
Search me and try me, Mas - ter, to -

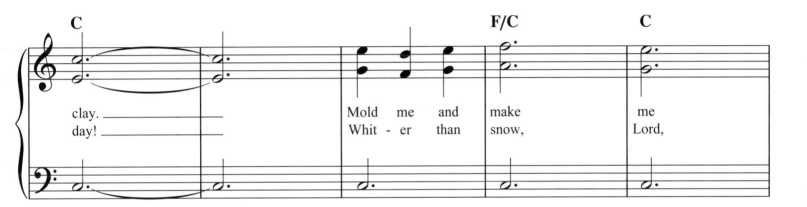

clay. Mold me and make me
day! Whit - er than snow, Lord,

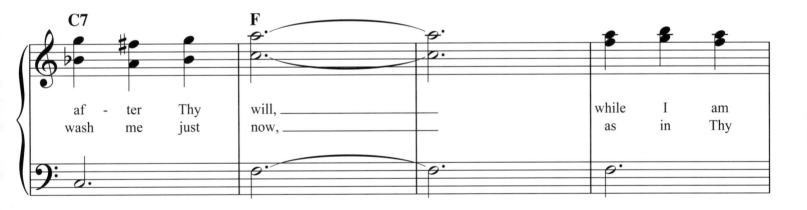

af - ter Thy will, while I am
wash me just now, as in Thy

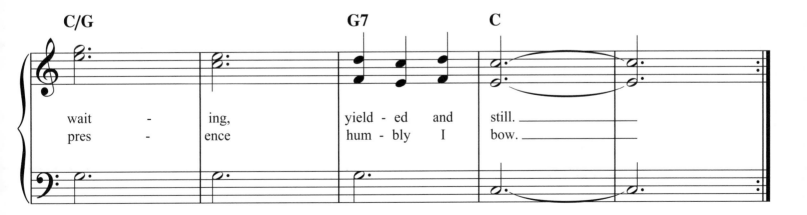

wait - ing, yield - ed and still.
pres - ence hum - bly I bow.

HOLY, HOLY, HOLY

Text by REGINALD HEBER
Music by JOHN B. DYKES

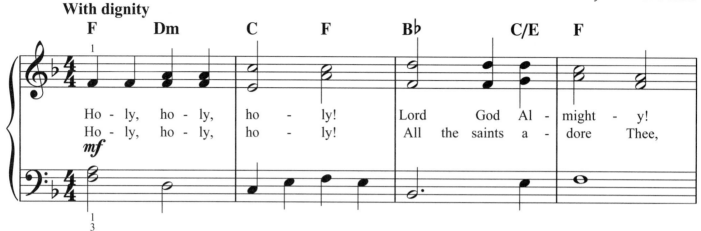

With dignity

Holy, holy, holy! Lord God Al - might - y!
Ho - ly, ho - ly, ho - ly! All the saints a - dore Thee,

Ear - ly in the morn - ing our song shall rise to Thee.
cast - ing down their gold - en crowns a - round the glass - y sea.

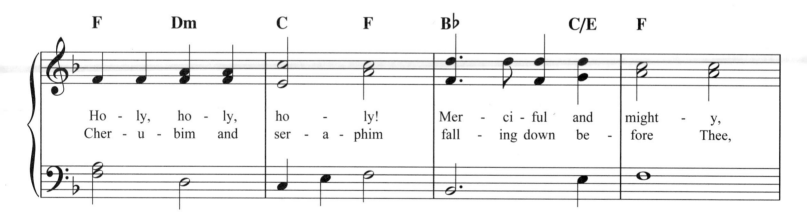

Ho - ly, ho - ly, ho - ly! Mer - ci - ful and might - y,
Cher - u - bim and ser - a - phim fall - ing down be - fore Thee,

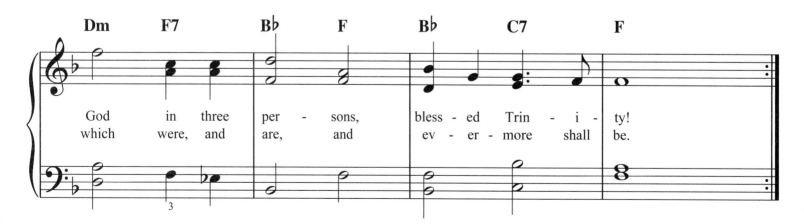

God in three per - sons, bless - ed Trin - i - ty!
which were, and are, and ev - er - more shall be.

JESUS LOVES ME

Words by ANNA B. WARNER
Music by WILLIAM B. BRADBURY

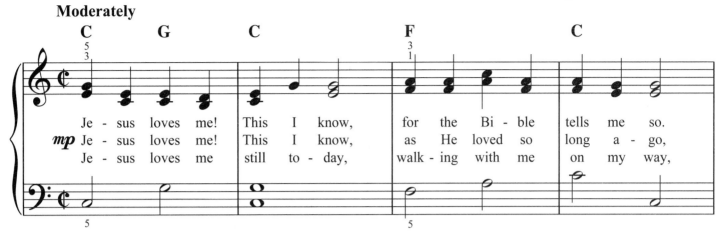

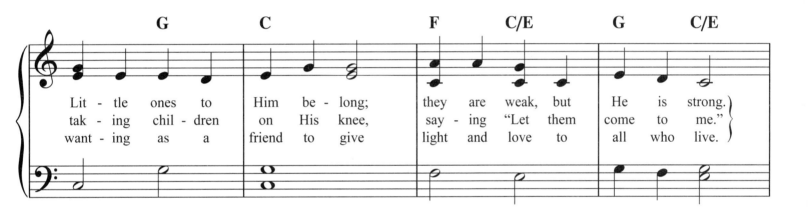

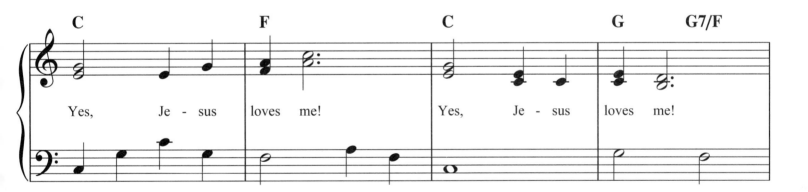

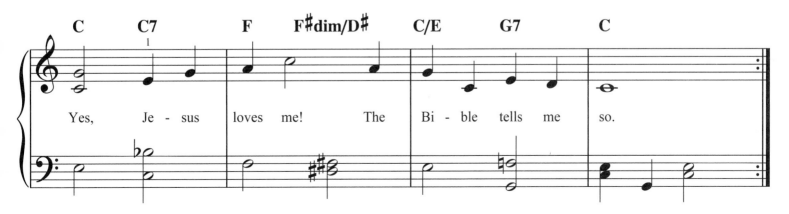

HOW FIRM A FOUNDATION

Words from JOHN RIPPON'S *A Selection of Hymns*
Early American Melody

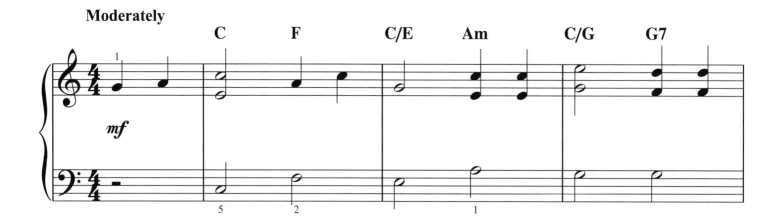

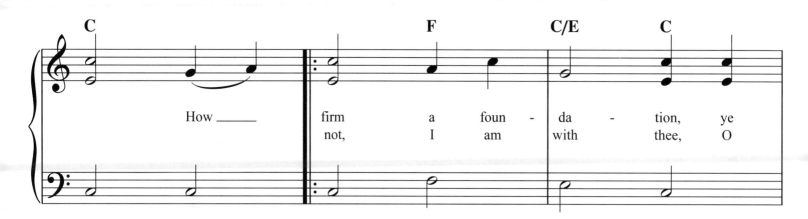

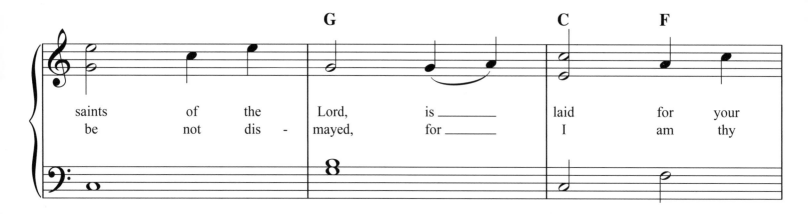

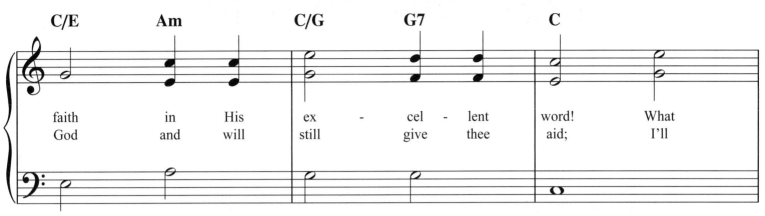

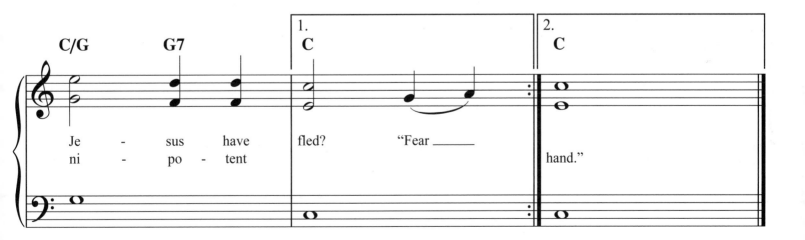

I AM THINE, O LORD

Words by FANNY J. CROSBY
Music by WILLIAM H. DOANE

Moderately fast

I am Thine, O Lord, I have heard Thy voice, and it
crate me now to Thy ser - vice, Lord, by the

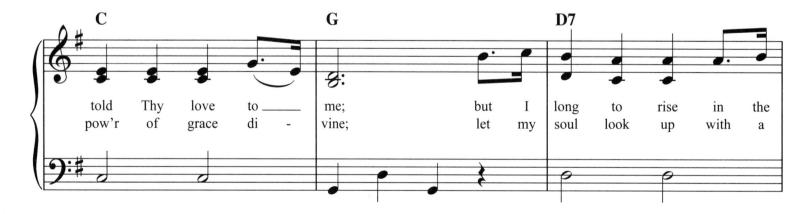

told Thy love to _____ me; but I long to rise in the
pow'r of grace di - vine; let my soul look up with a

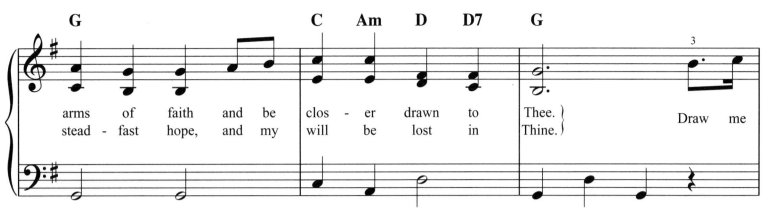

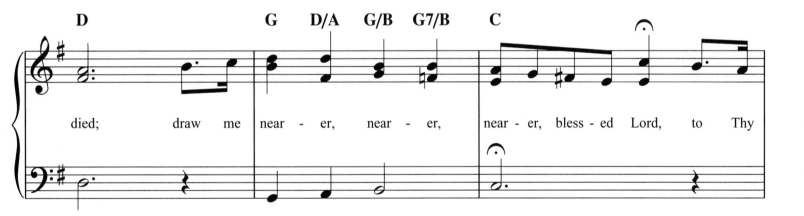

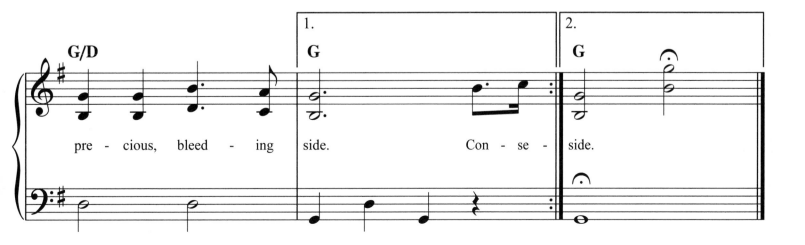

I LOVE TO TELL THE STORY

Words by A. CATHERINE HANKEY
Music by WILLIAM G. FISCHER

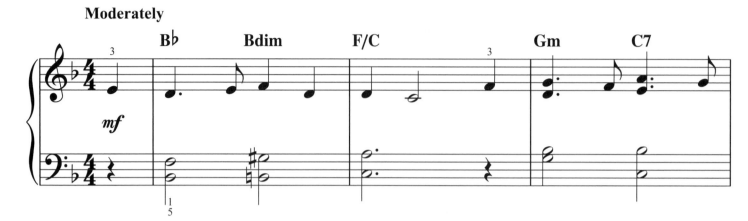

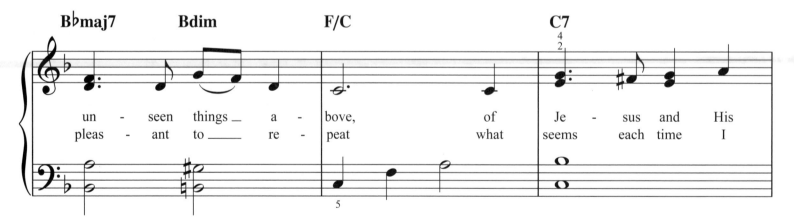

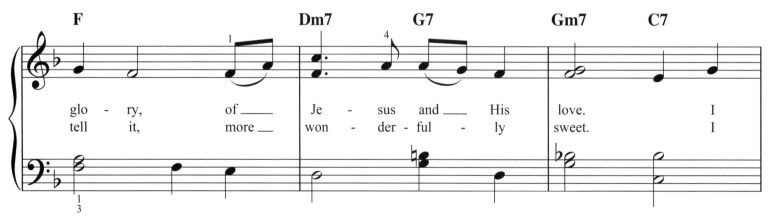

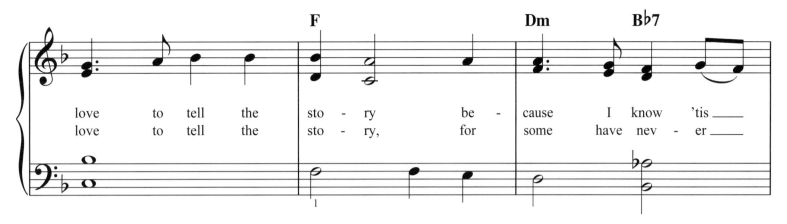

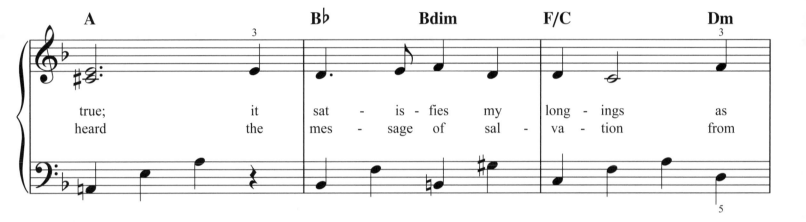

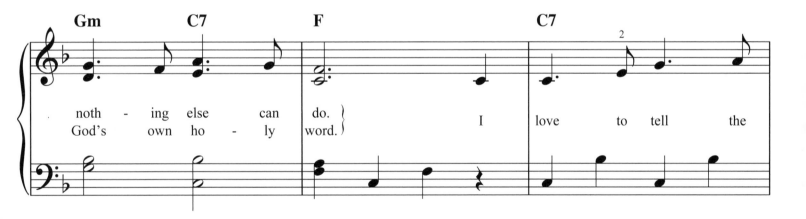

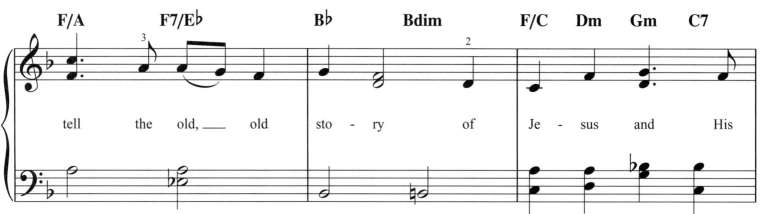

F/A **F7/E♭** **B♭** **Bdim** **F/C Dm Gm C7**

tell the old, — old sto - ry of Je - sus and His

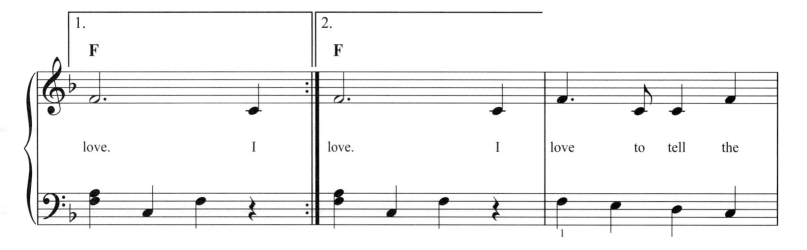

1.
F

love. I

2.
F

love. I love to tell the

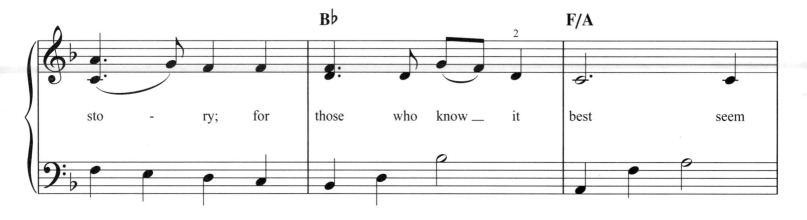

B♭ **F/A**

sto - ry; for those who know — it best seem

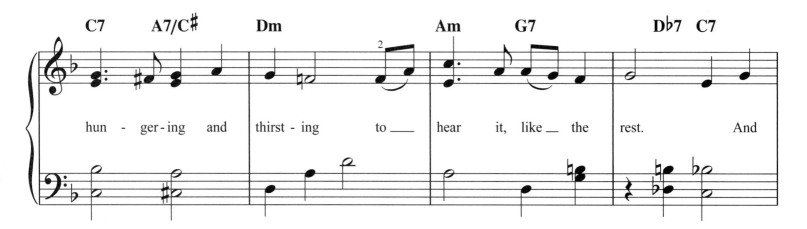

C7 **A7/C♯** **Dm** **Am** **G7** **D♭7 C7**

hun - ger - ing and thirst - ing to — hear it, like — the rest. And

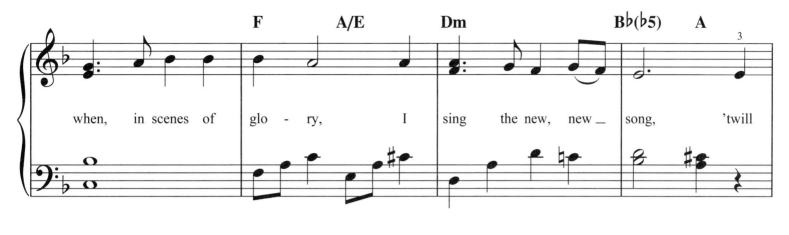

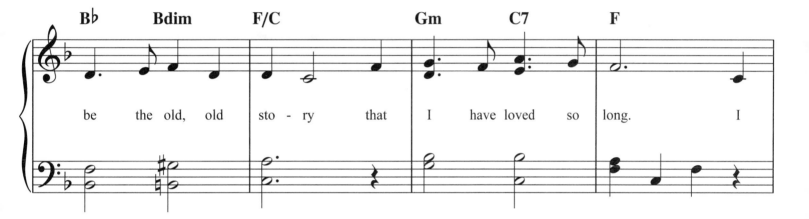

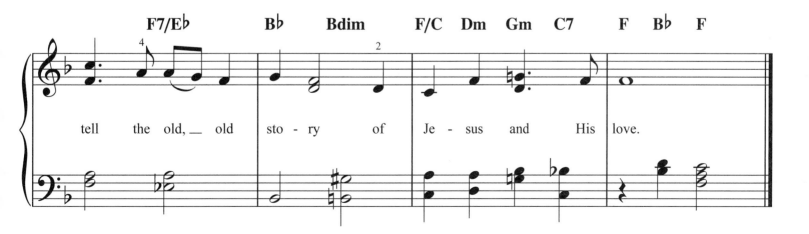

I NEED THEE EVERY HOUR

Words by ANNIE S. HAWKS
Music by ROBERT LOWRY

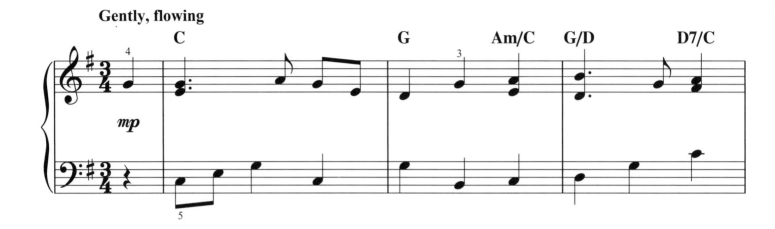

I
need Thee ev - 'ry hour, most
need Thee ev - 'ry hour, most stay

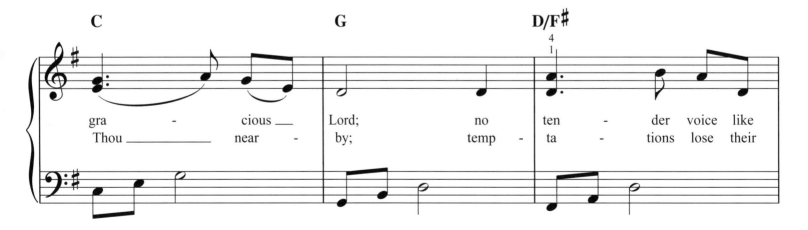

gra - cious ___ Lord; no ten - der voice like
Thou ___ near - by; temp - ta - tions lose their

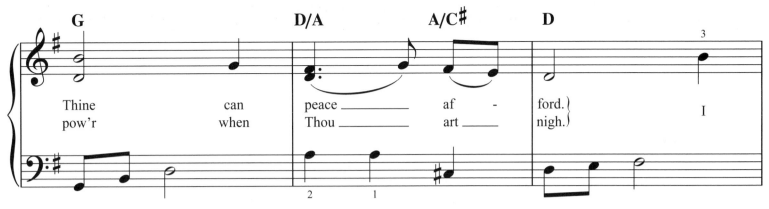

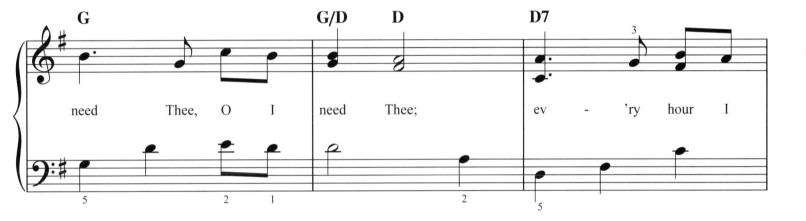

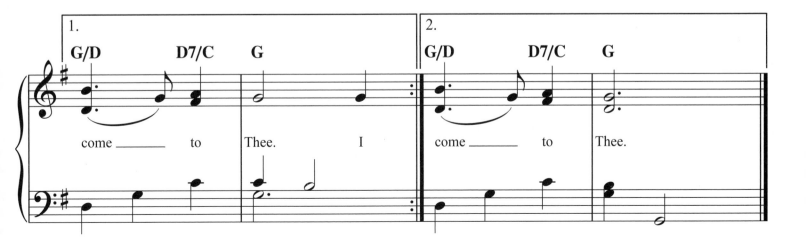

I SING THE MIGHTY POWER OF GOD

Words by ISAAC WATTS
Music from *Gesangbuch der Herzogl*

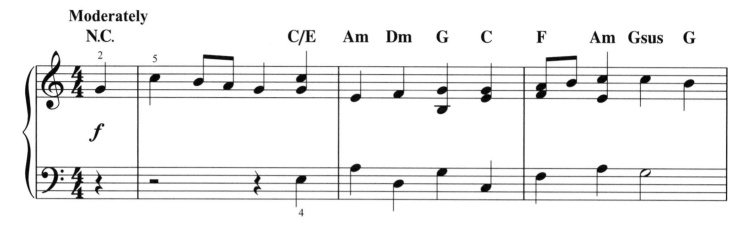

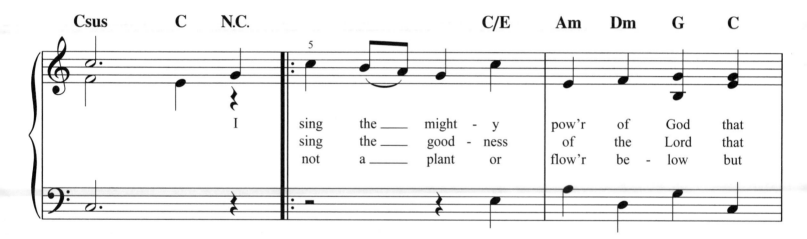

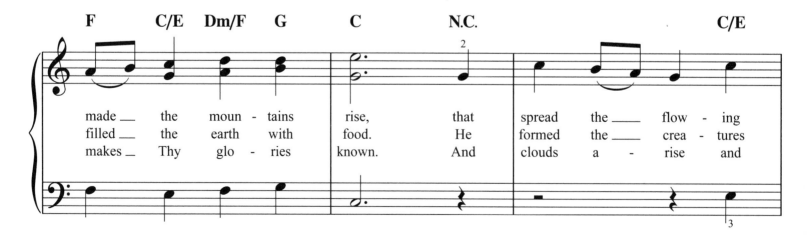

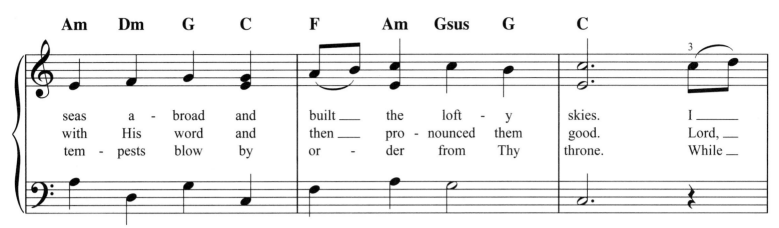

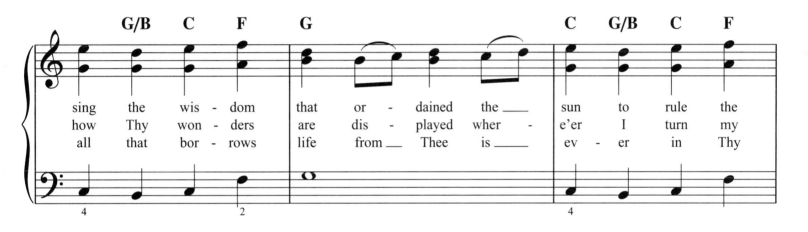

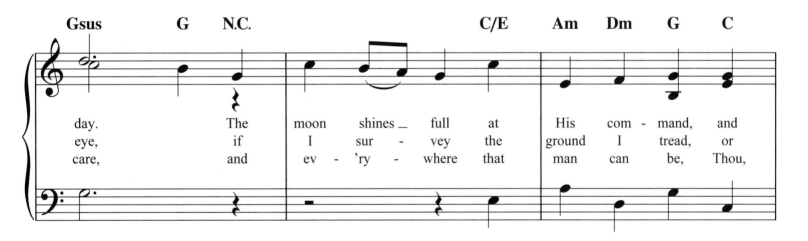

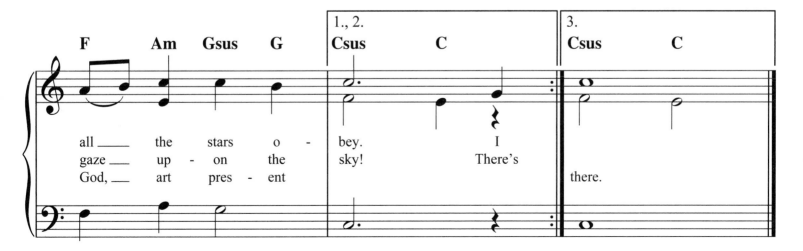

I SURRENDER ALL

Words by J.W. VAN DEVENTER
Music by W.S. WEEDEN

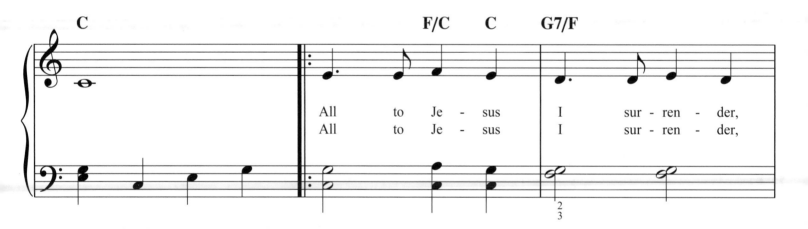

All to Je - sus I sur - ren - der,
All to Je - sus I sur - ren - der,

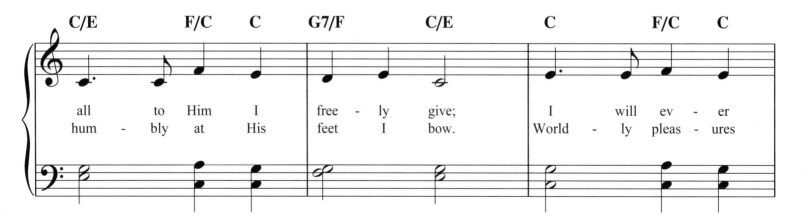

all to Him I free - ly give;
hum - bly at His feet I bow.

I will ev - er
World - ly pleas - ures

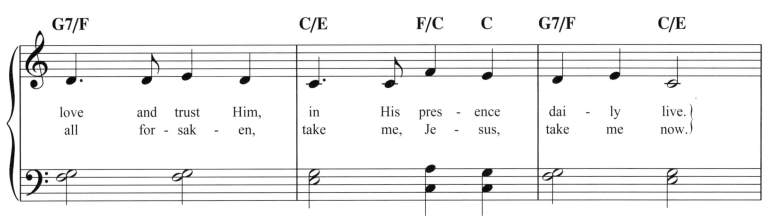

love   and trust Him,   in   His pres - ence   dai - ly live.
all   for - sak - en,   take   me, Je - sus,   take me now.

I   sur - ren - der   all,   I   sur - ren - der

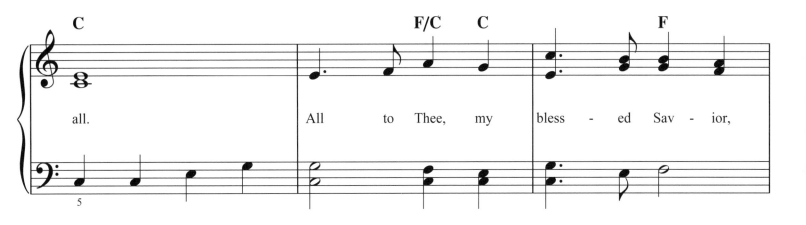

all.   All   to Thee, my   bless - ed Sav - ior,

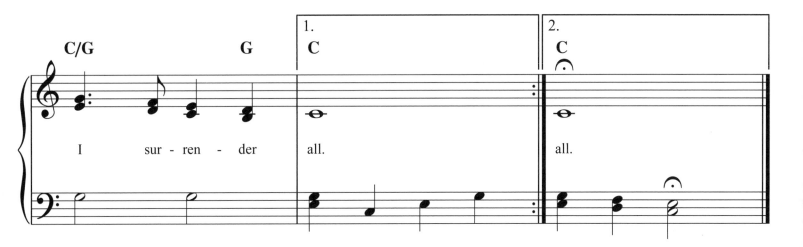

I   sur - ren - der   all.   all.

IMMORTAL, INVISIBLE

Words by WALTER CHALMERS SMITH
Traditional Welsh Melody
From John Roberts' *Canaidau y Cyssegr*

With strength

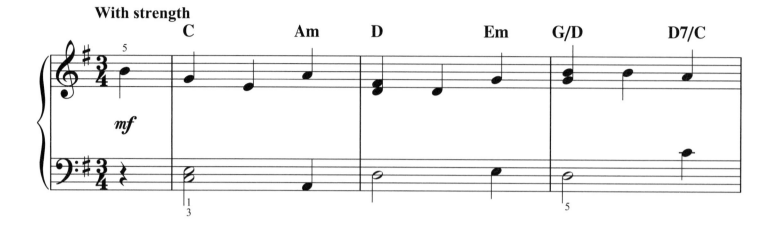

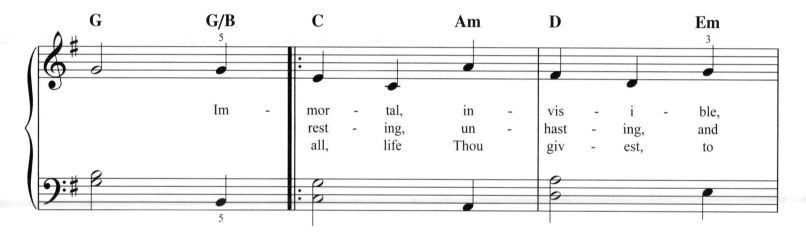

Im - mor - tal, in - vis - i - ble,
rest - ing, un - hast - ing, and
all, life Thou giv - est, to

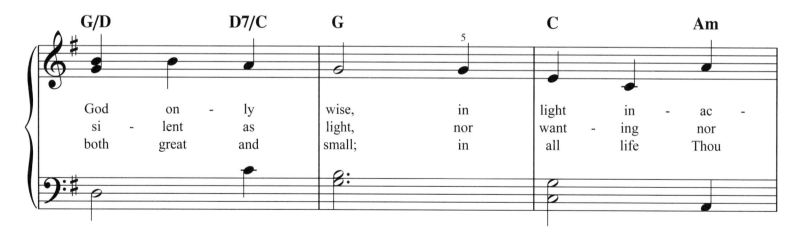

God on - ly wise, in light in - ac -
si - lent as light, nor want - ing nor
both great and small; in all life Thou

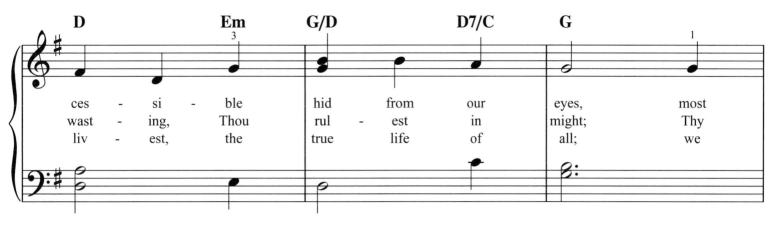

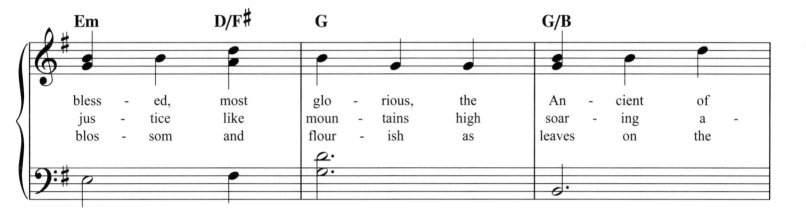

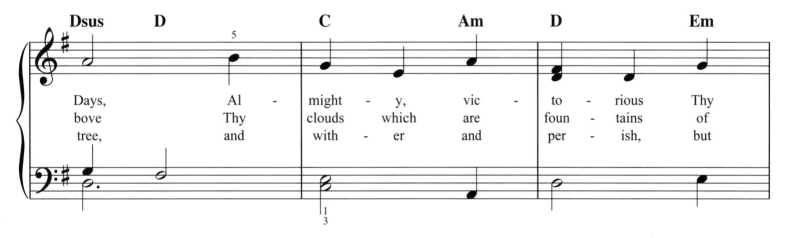

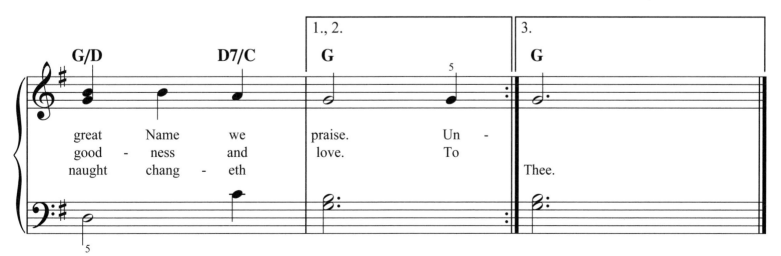

IT IS WELL WITH MY SOUL

Words by HORATIO G. SPAFFORD
Music by PHILIP P. BLISS

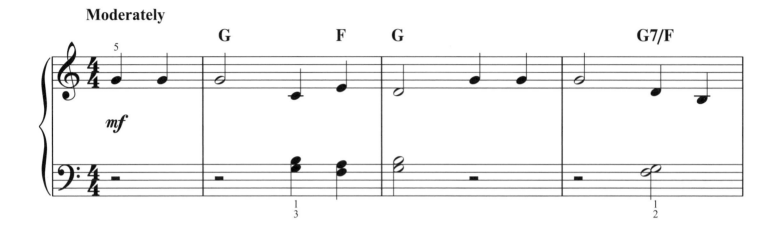

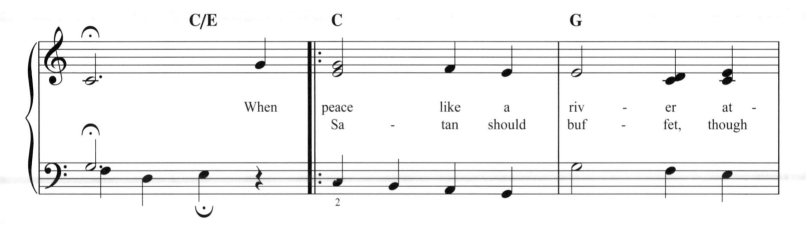

When peace like a riv - er at -
Sa - tan should buf - fet, though

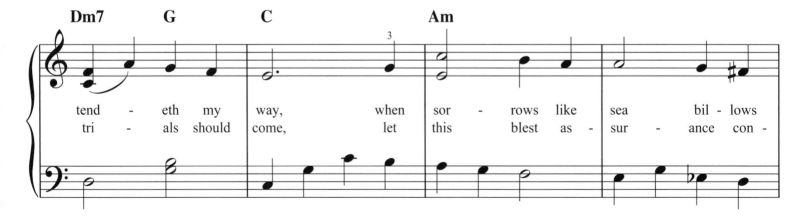

tend - eth my way, when sor - rows like sea bil - lows
tri - als should come, let this blest as - sur - ance con -

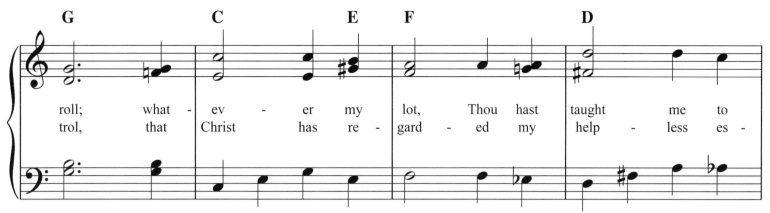

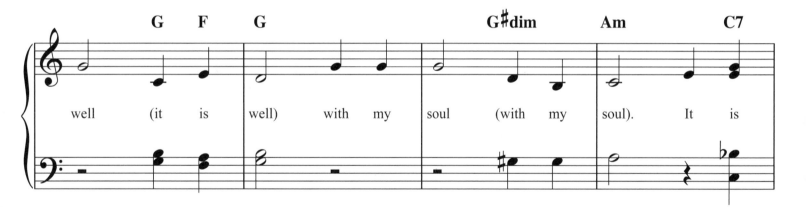

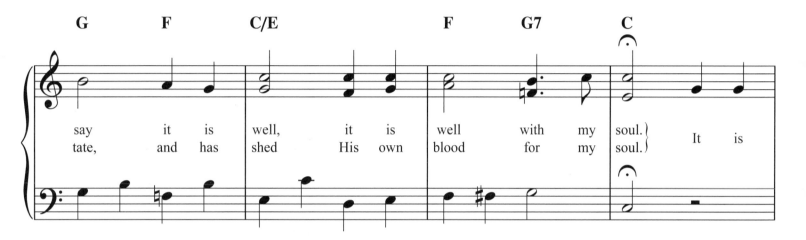

JESUS PAID IT ALL

Words by ELVINA M. HALL
Music by JOHN T. GRAPE

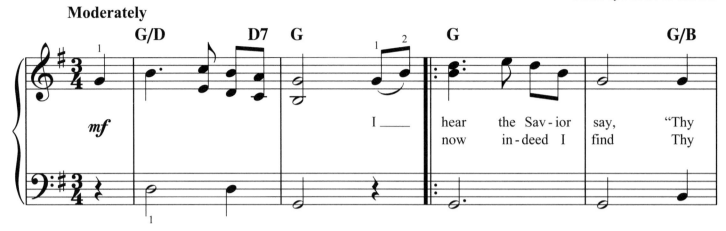

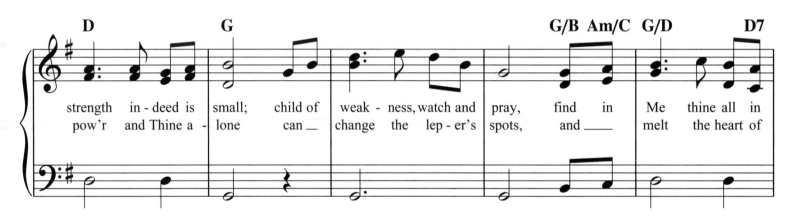

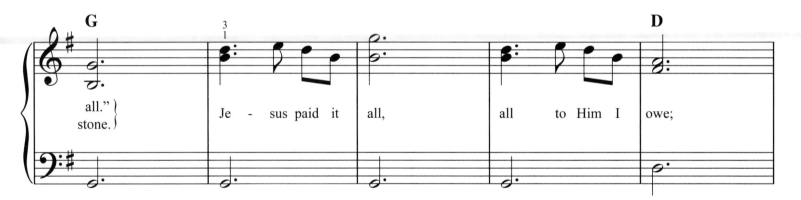

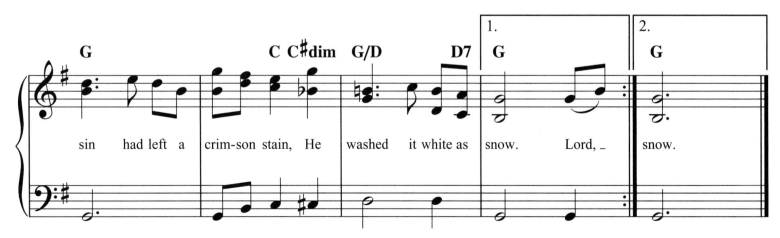

NEARER, MY GOD, TO THEE

Words by SARAH F. ADAMS
Based on Genesis 28:10-22
Music by LOWELL MASON

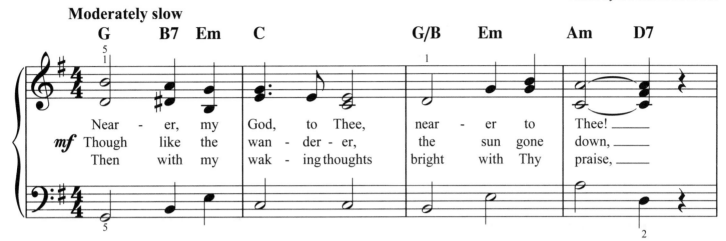

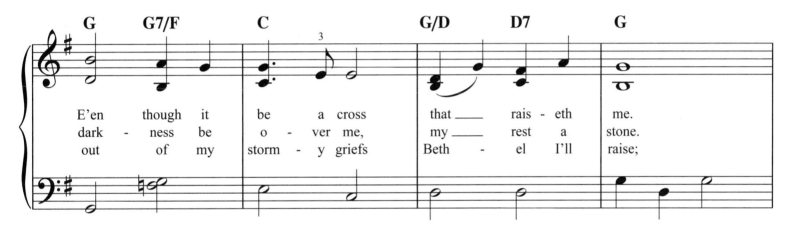

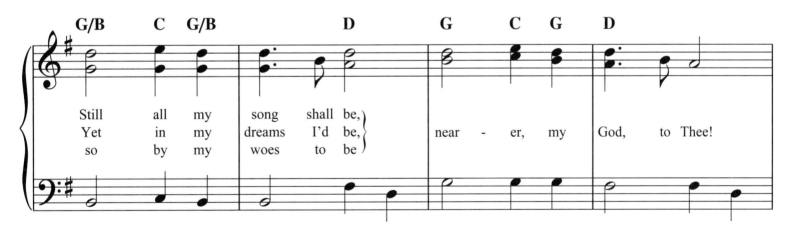

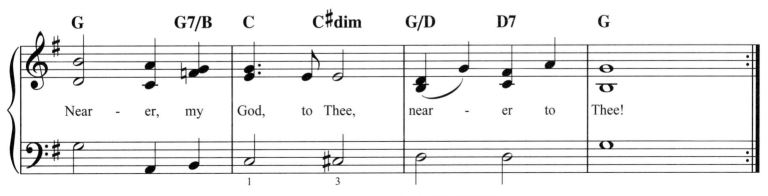

JESUS SHALL REIGN

Words by ISAAC WATTS
Music by JOHN HATTON

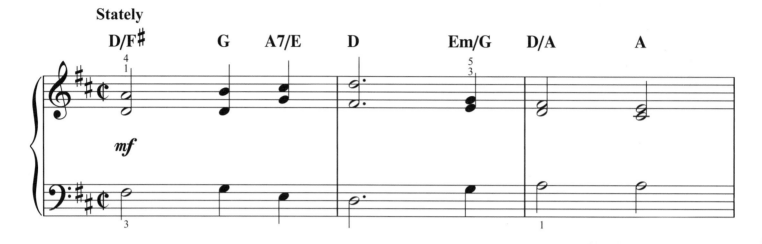

Je - sus shall reign where -
To Him shall end - less _____

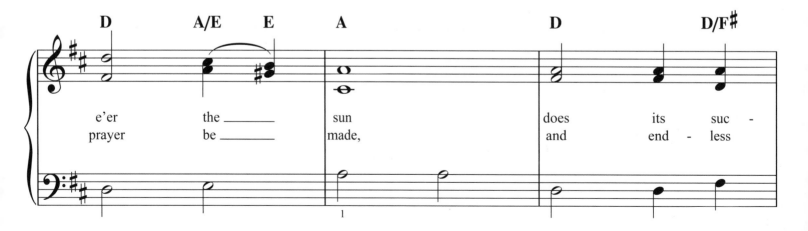

e'er the _____ sun made, does its suc -
prayer be _____ made, and end - less

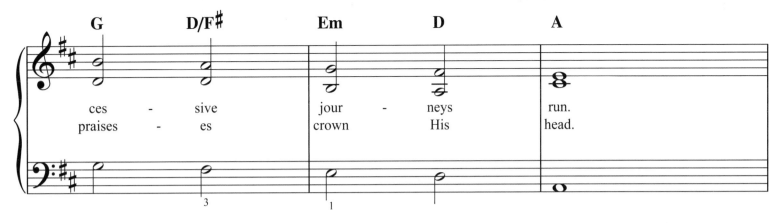

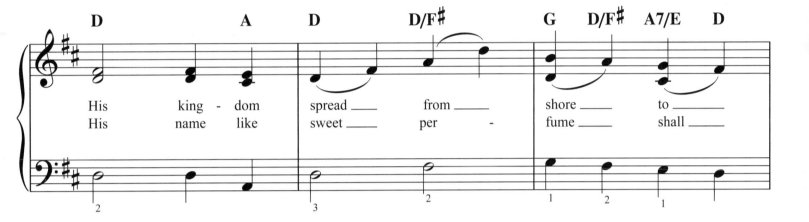

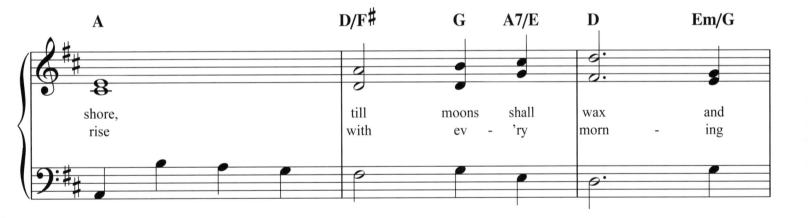

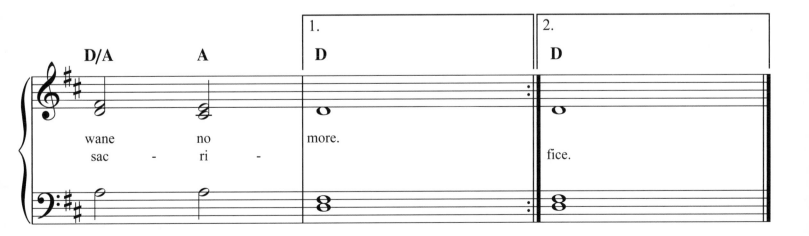

JOYFUL, JOYFUL, WE ADORE THEE

Words by HENRY VAN DYKE
Music by LUDWIG VAN BEETHOVEN,
melody from *Ninth Symphony*
Adapted by EDWARD HODGES

Brightly

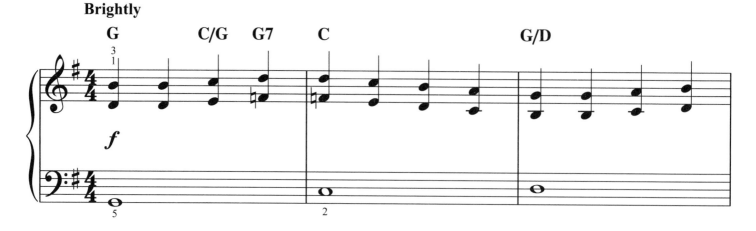

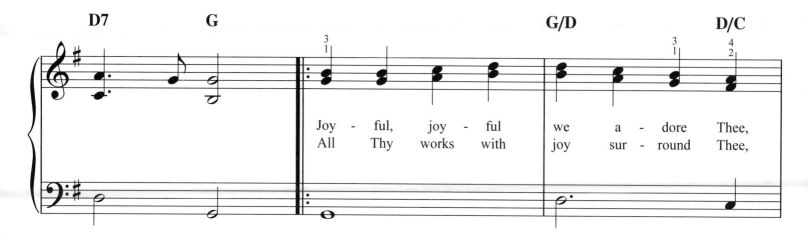

Joy - ful, joy - ful | we a - dore Thee,
All Thy works with | joy sur - round Thee,

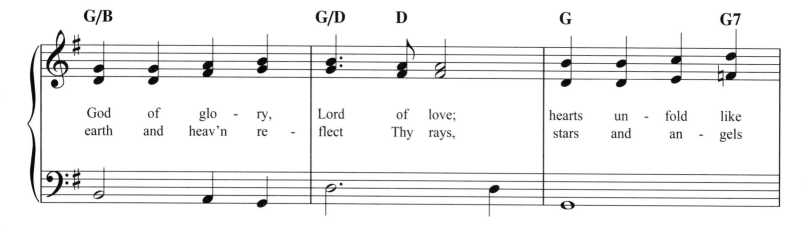

God of glo - ry, | Lord of love; | hearts un - fold like
earth and heav'n re - | flect Thy rays, | stars and an - gels

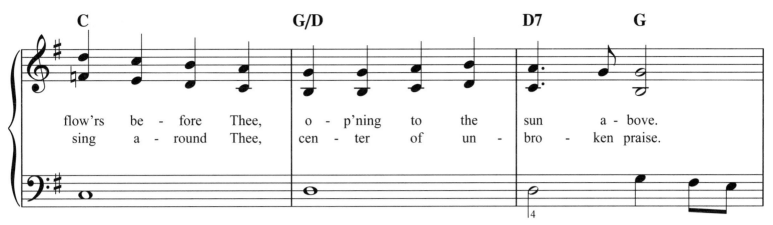

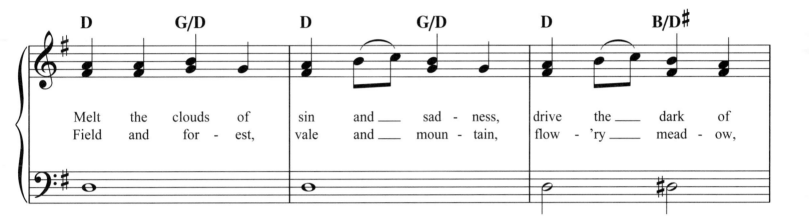

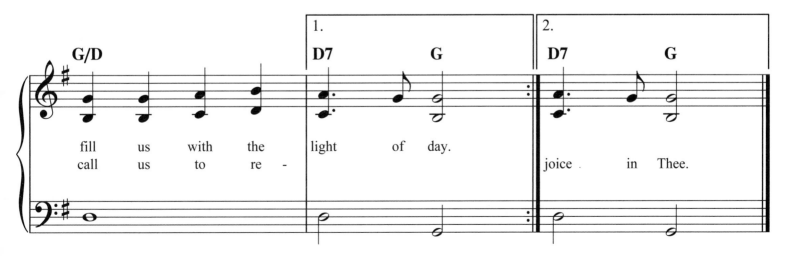

LEANING ON THE EVERLASTING ARMS

Words by ELISHA A. HOFFMAN
Music by ANTHONY J. SHOWALTER

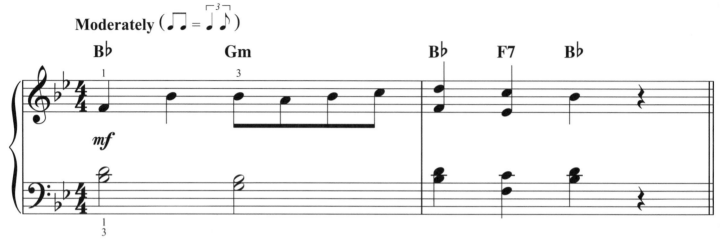

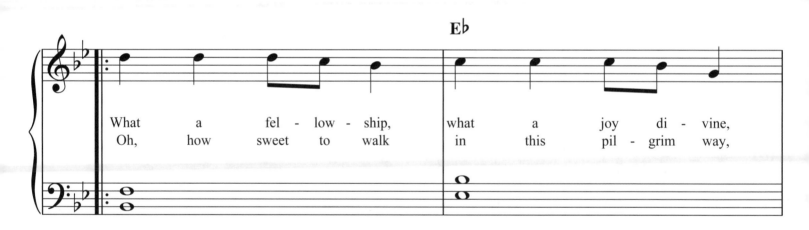

What a fel - low - ship, what a joy di - vine,
Oh, how sweet to walk in this pil - grim way,

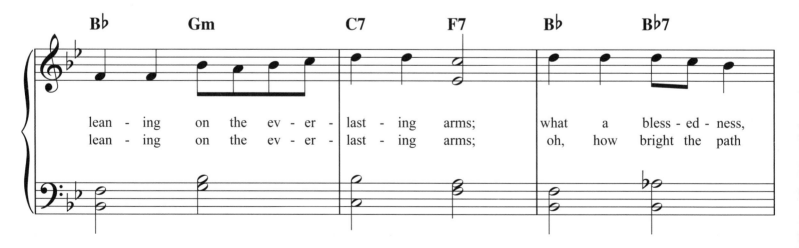

lean - ing on the ev - er - last - ing arms; what a bless - ed - ness,
lean - ing on the ev - er - last - ing arms; oh, how bright the path

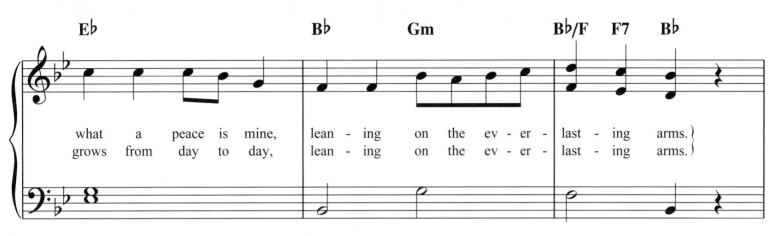

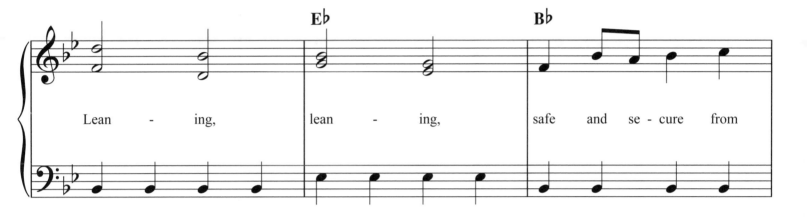

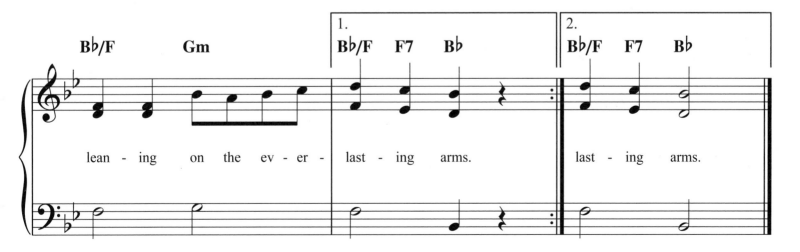

A MIGHTY FORTRESS IS OUR GOD

Words and Music by MARTIN LUTHER
Translated by FREDERICK H. HEDGE
Based on Psalm 46

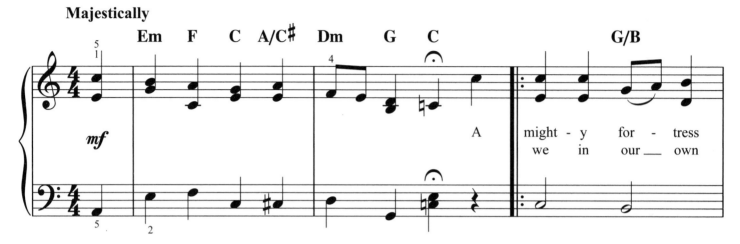

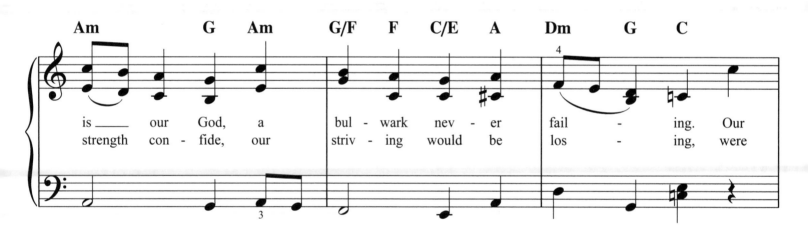

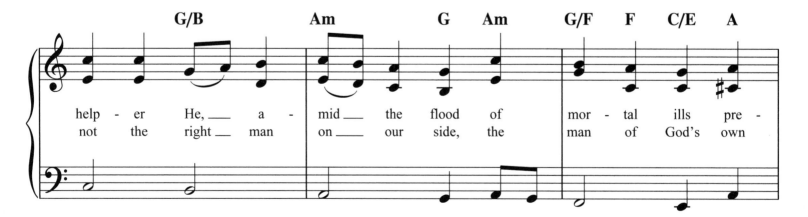

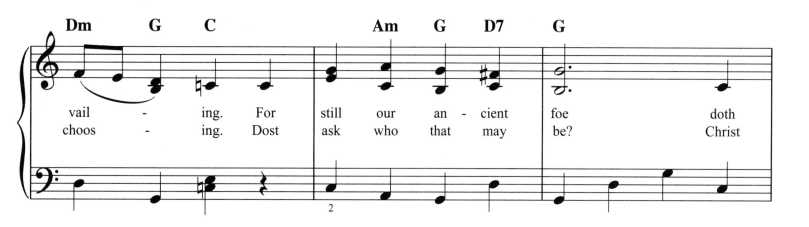

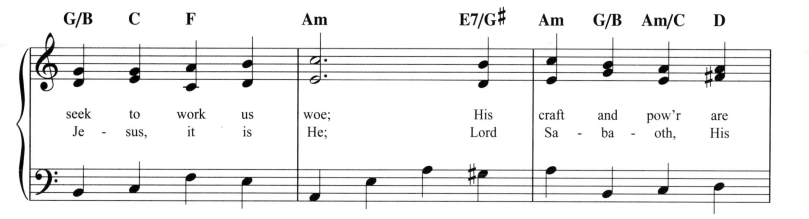

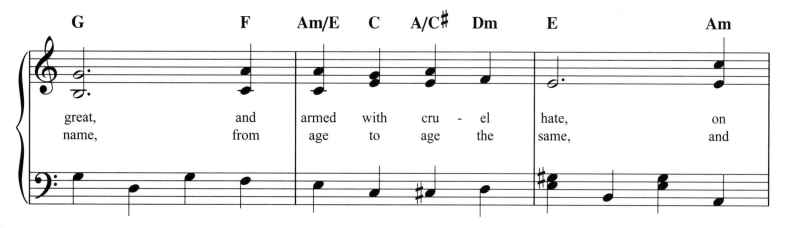

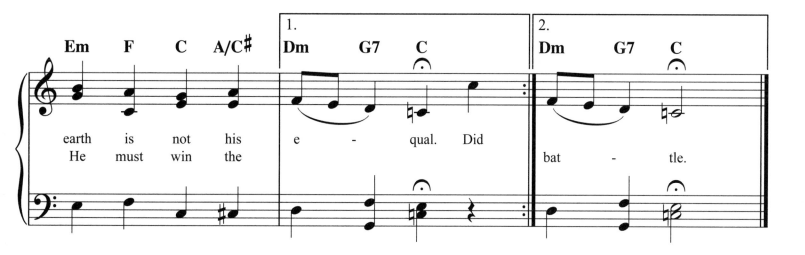

MY FAITH LOOKS UP TO THEE

Words by RAY PALMER
Music by LOWELL MASON

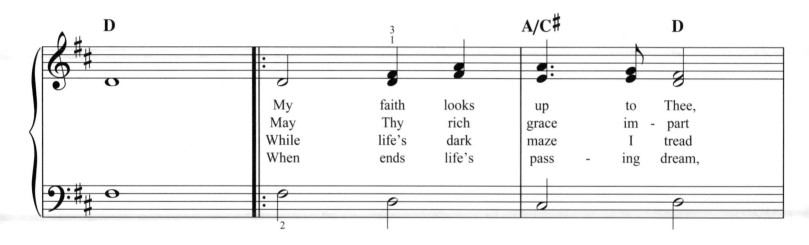

My faith looks up to Thee,
May Thy rich grace im - part
While life's dark maze I tread
When ends life's pass - ing dream,

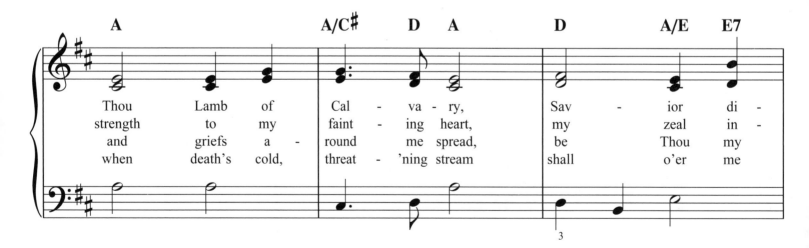

Thou Lamb of Cal - va - ry,
strength to my faint - ing heart,
and griefs a - round me spread,
when death's cold, threat - 'ning stream

Sav - ior di -
my zeal in -
be Thou my
shall o'er me

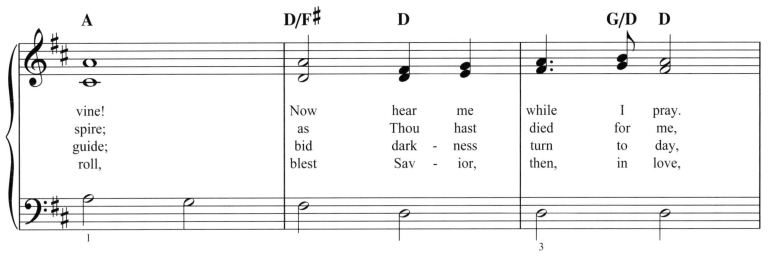

vine! | Now hear me | while I pray.
spire; | as Thou hast | died for me,
guide; | bid dark - ness | turn to day,
roll, | blest Sav - ior, | then, in love,

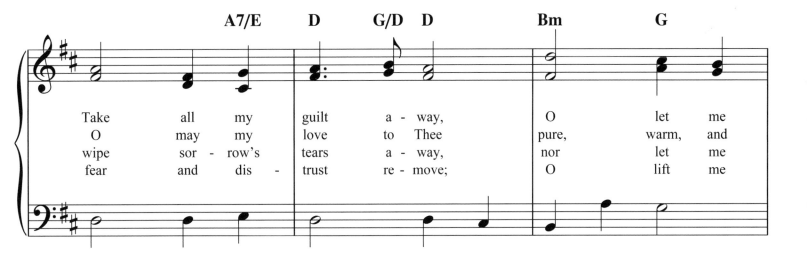

Take all my | guilt a - way, | O let me
O may my | love to Thee | pure, warm, and
wipe sor - row's | tears a - way, | nor let me
fear and dis - | trust re - move; | O lift me

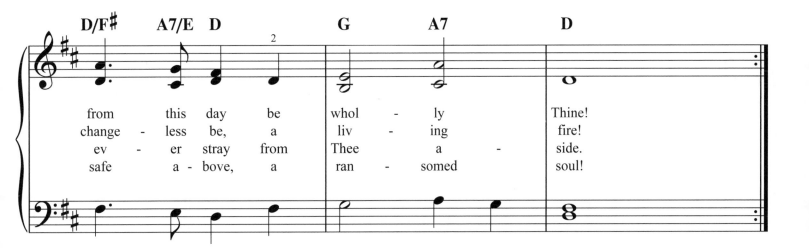

from this day be | whol - ly | Thine!
change - less be, a | liv - ing | fire!
ev - er stray from | Thee a - | side.
safe a - bove, a | ran - somed | soul!

O FOR A THOUSAND TONGUES TO SING

Words by CHARLES WESLEY
Music by CARL G. GLASER
Arranged by LOWELL MASON

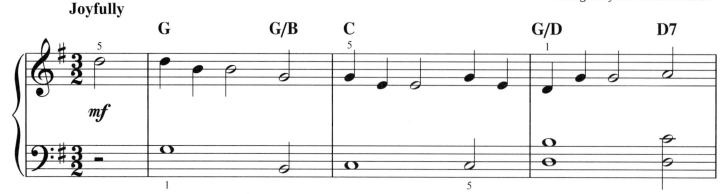

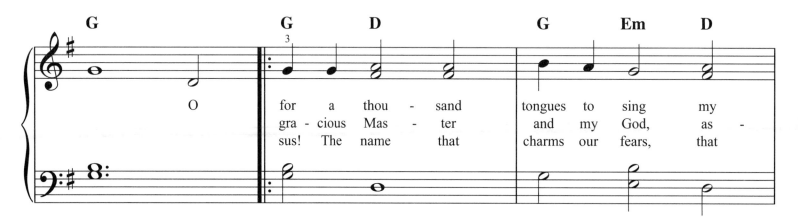

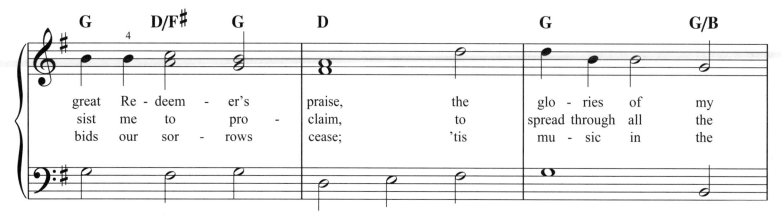

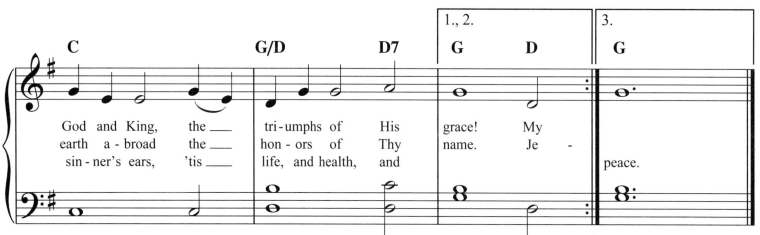

PRAISE GOD, FROM WHOM ALL BLESSINGS FLOW

Words by THOMAS KEN
Music Attributed to LOUIS BOURGEOIS

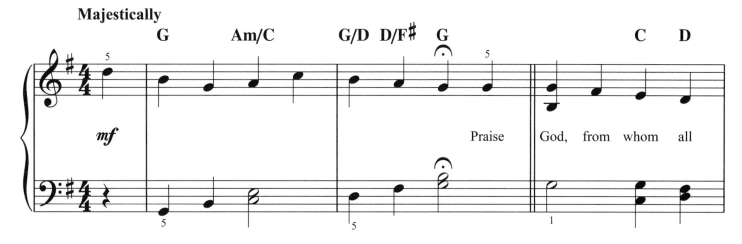

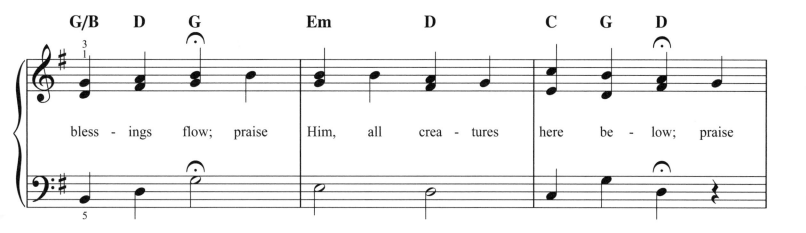

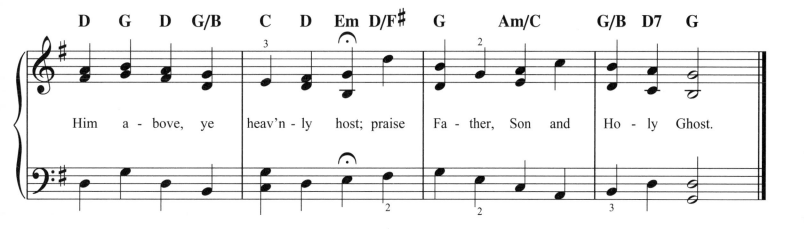

O MASTER, LET ME WALK WITH THEE

Words by WASHINGTON GLADDEN
Music by H. PERCY SMITH

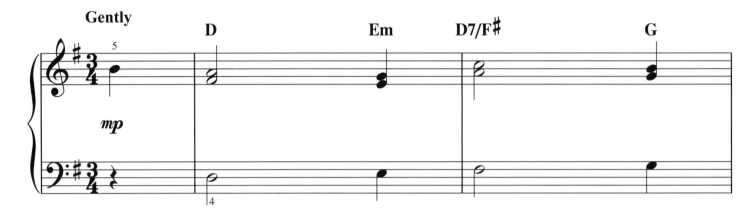

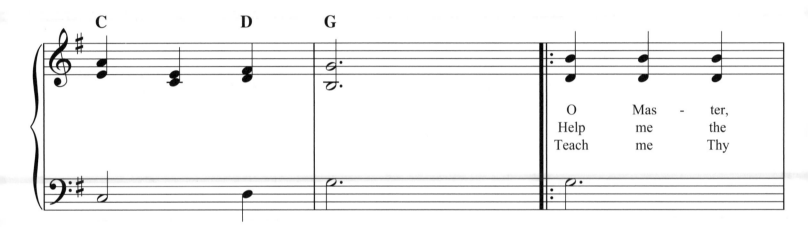

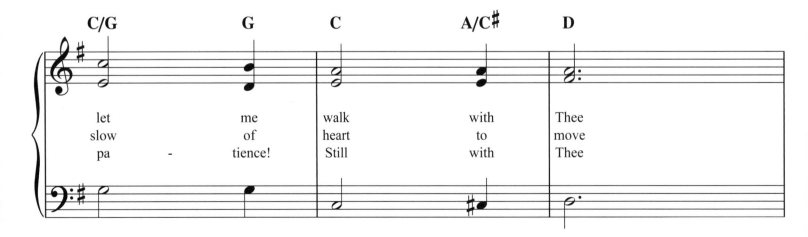

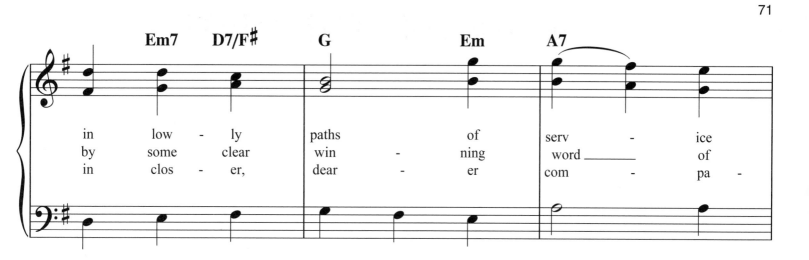

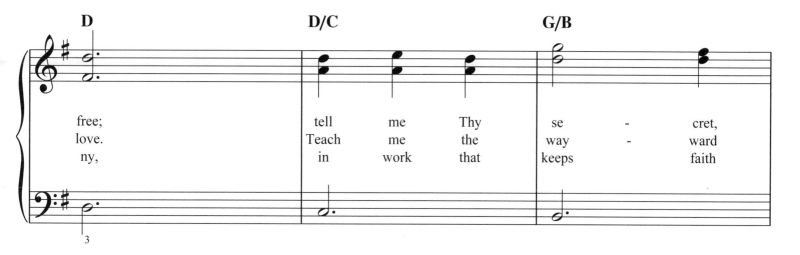

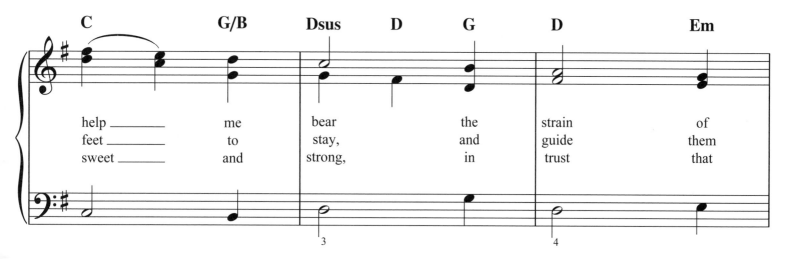

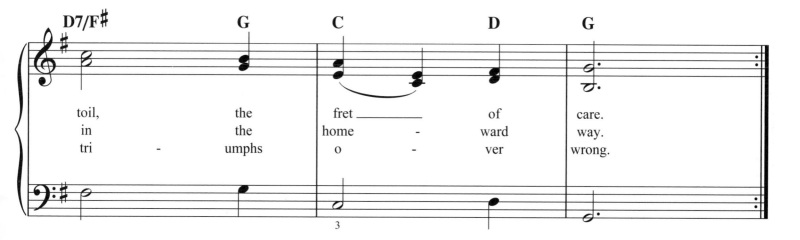

O WORSHIP THE KING

Words by ROBERT GRANT
Music attributed to JOHANN MICHAEL HAYDN
Arranged by WILLIAM GARDINER

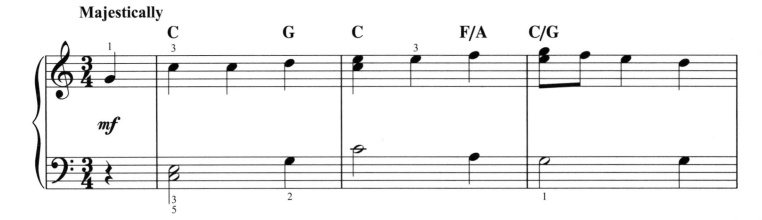

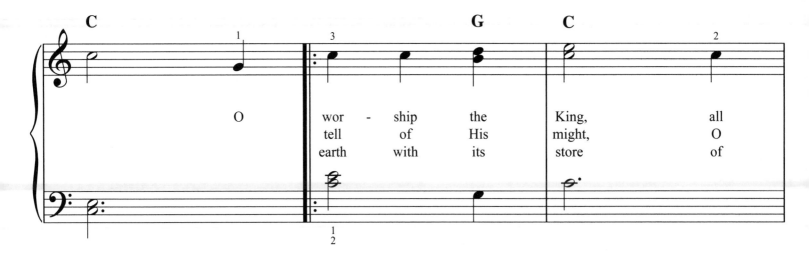

O wor - ship the King, all
tell of His might,
earth with its store O of

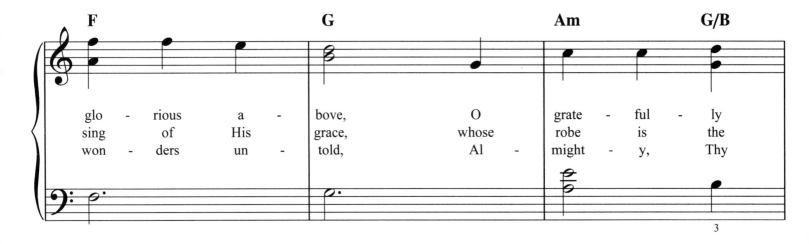

glo - rious a - bove, O grate - ful - ly
sing of His grace, whose robe is the
won - ders un - told, Al - might - y, Thy

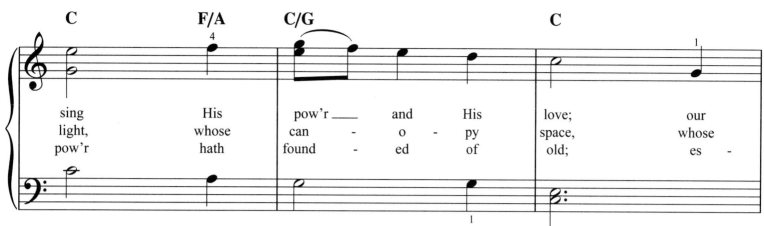

C   F/A   C/G   C

sing   His   pow'r ____ and   His   love;   our
light,   whose   can - o - py   space,   whose
pow'r   hath   found - ed   of   old;   es -

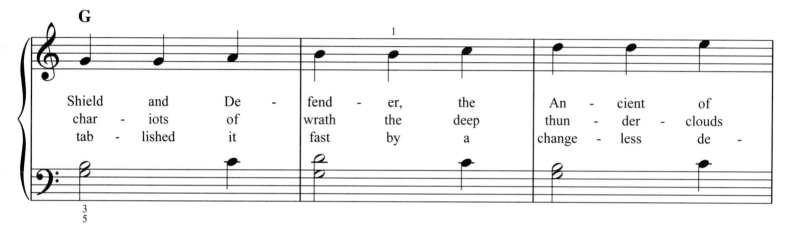

G

Shield   and   De - fend - er,   the   An - cient   of
char - iots   of   wrath   the   deep   thun - der - clouds
tab - lished   of   it   fast   by   a   change - less   de -

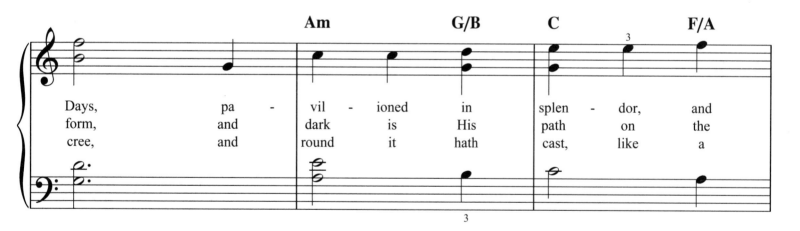

Am   G/B   C   F/A

Days,   pa - vil - ioned   in   splen - dor,   and
form,   and   dark   is   His   path   on   the
cree,   and   round   it   hath   cast,   like   a

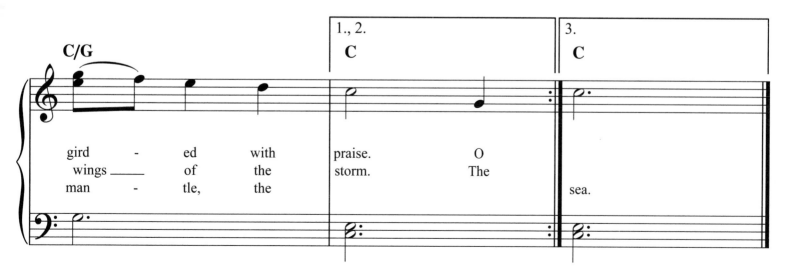

C/G   1., 2.   3.
                C   C

gird - ed   with   praise.   O
wings ___ of   the   storm.   The   sea.
man - tle,   the

PRAISE TO THE LORD, THE ALMIGHTY

Words by JOACHIM NEANDER
Translated by CATHERINE WINKWORTH
Music from *Erneuerten Gesangbuch*

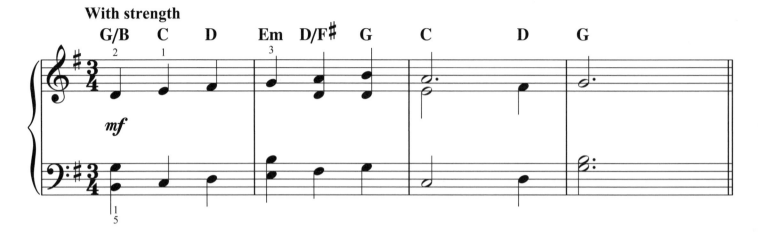

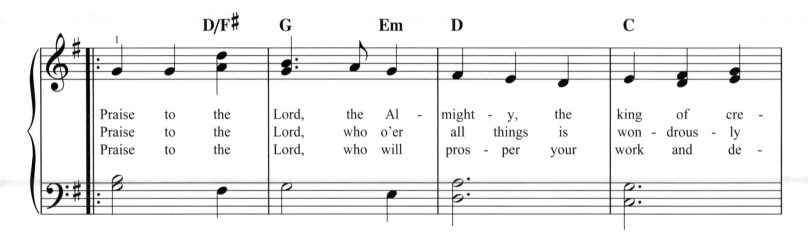

Praise to the Lord, the Al - might - y, the king of cre -
Praise to the Lord, who o'er all things is won - drous - ly
Praise to the Lord, who will pros - per your work and de -

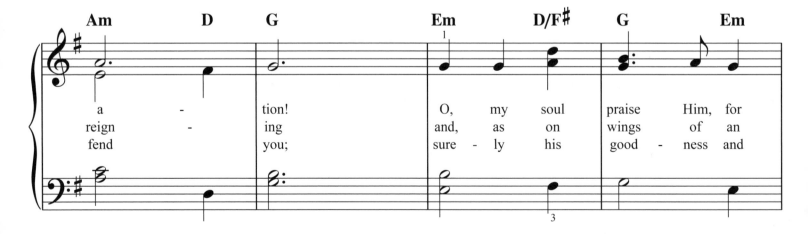

a - tion!
reign - ing
fend you;

O, my soul praise Him, for
and, as on wings of an
sure - ly his good - ness and

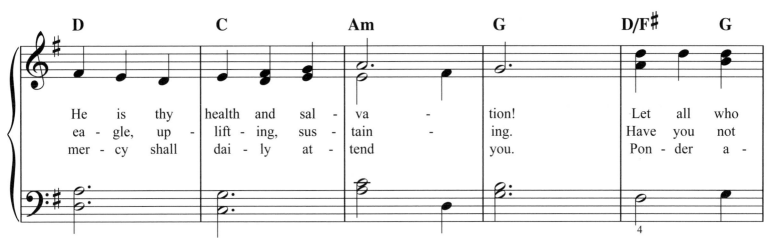

He is thy health and sal - va - tion! Let all who
ea - gle, up - lift - ing, sus - tain - ing. Have you not
mer - cy shall dai - ly at - tend you. Pon - der a -

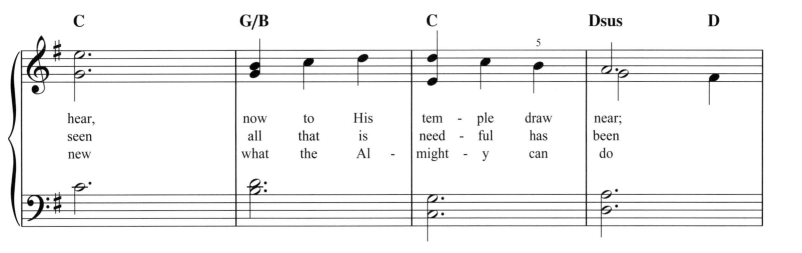

hear, now to His tem - ple draw near;
seen all that is need - ful has been
new what the Al - might - y can do

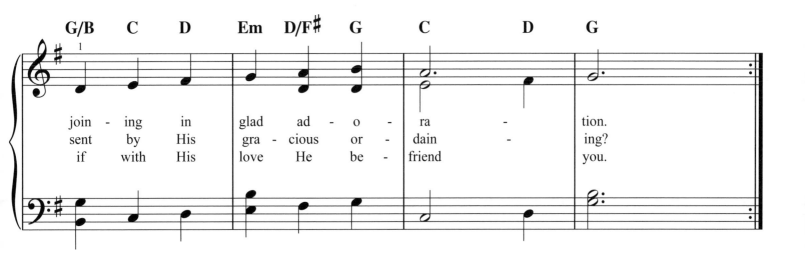

join - ing in glad ad - o - ra - tion.
sent by His gra - cious or - dain - ing?
if with His love He be - friend you.

ROCK OF AGES

Words by AUGUSTUS M. TOPLADY
V.1,2,4 altered by THOMAS COTTERILL
Music by THOMAS HASTINGS

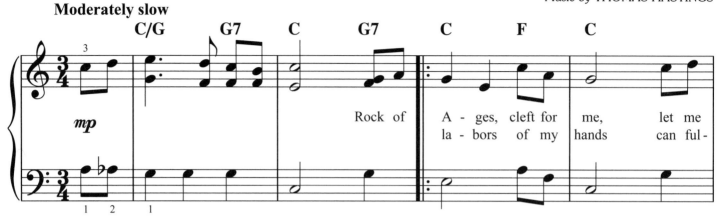

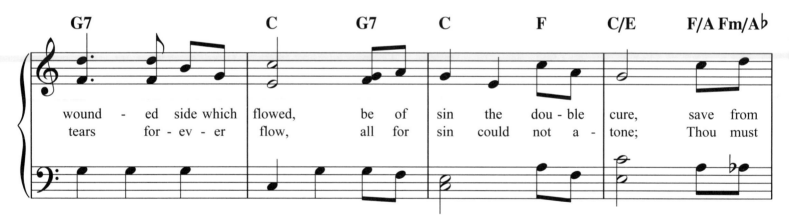

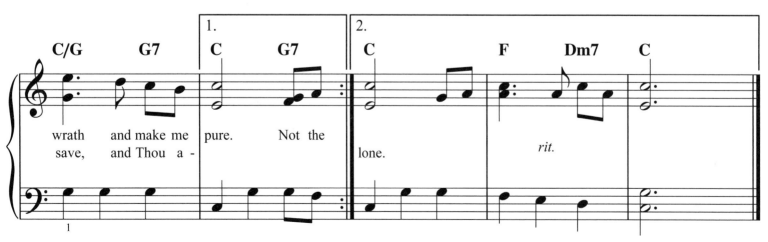

SOFTLY AND TENDERLY

Words and Music by
WILL L. THOMPSON

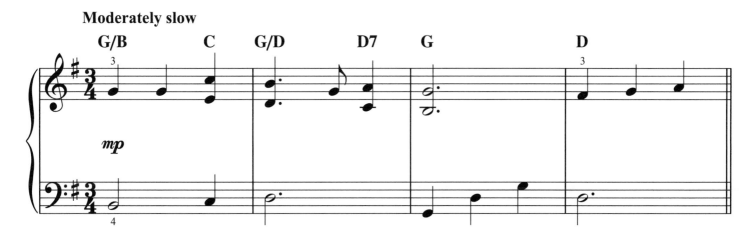

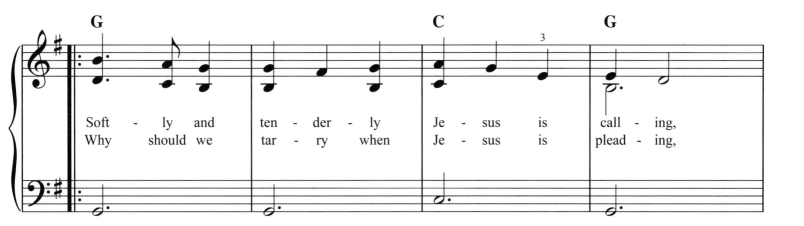

Soft - ly and ten - der - ly Je - sus is call - ing,
Why should we tar - ry when Je - sus is plead - ing,

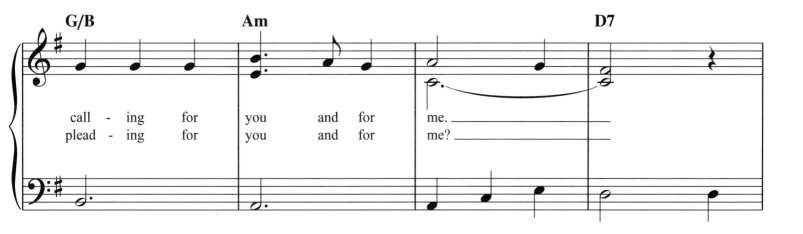

call - ing for you and for me.
plead - ing for you and for me?

78

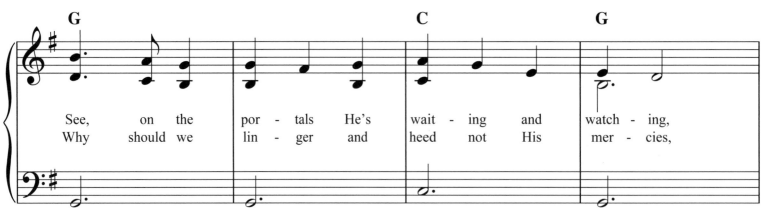

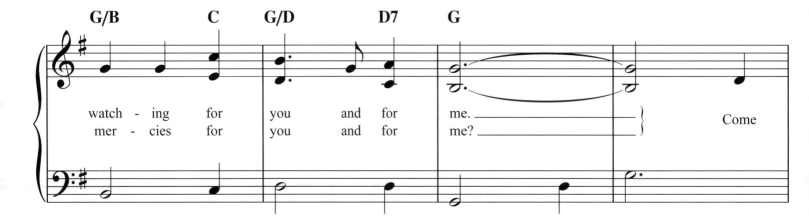

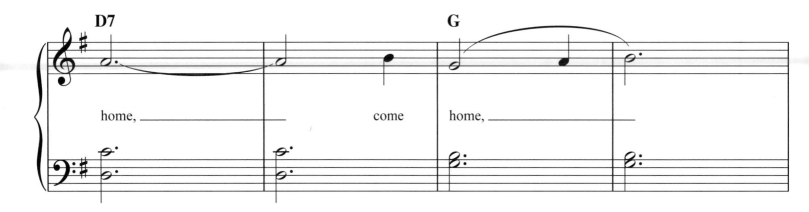

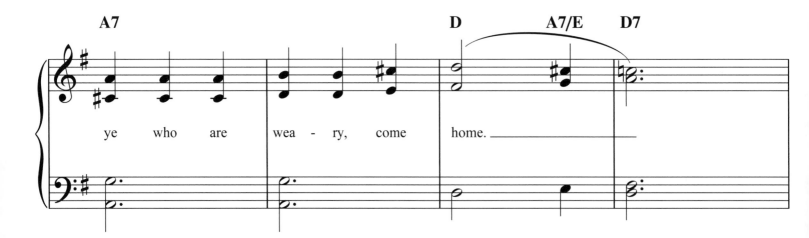

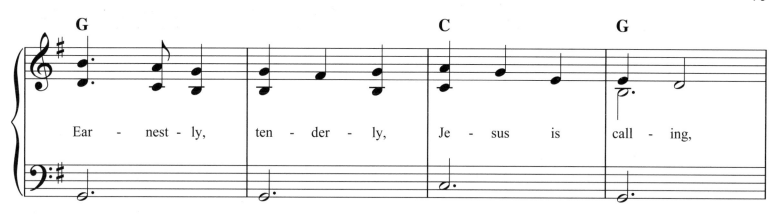

Ear - nest - ly, ten - der - ly, Je - sus is call - ing,

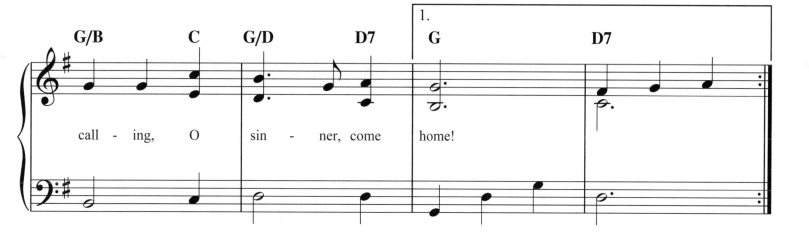

call - ing, O sin - ner, come home!

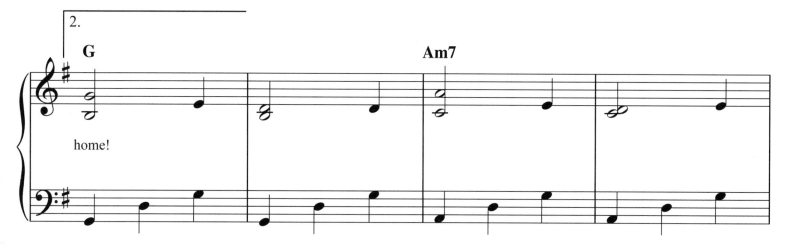

home!

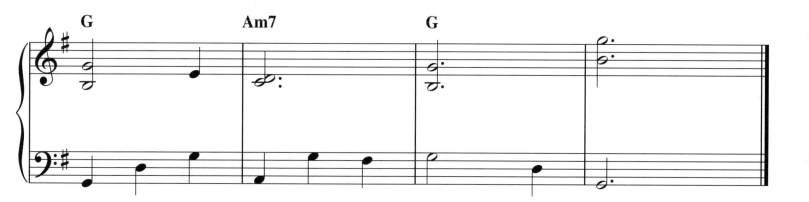

SAVIOR, LIKE A SHEPHERD LEAD US

Words from *Hymns For The Young*
Attributed to DOROTHY A. THRUPP
Music by WILLIAM B. BRADBURY

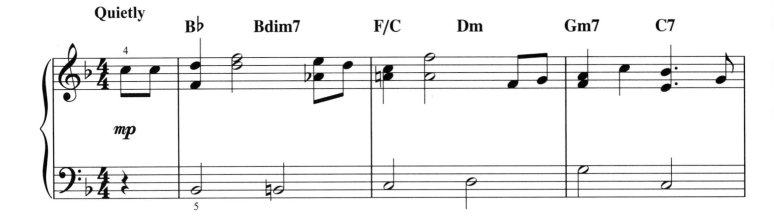

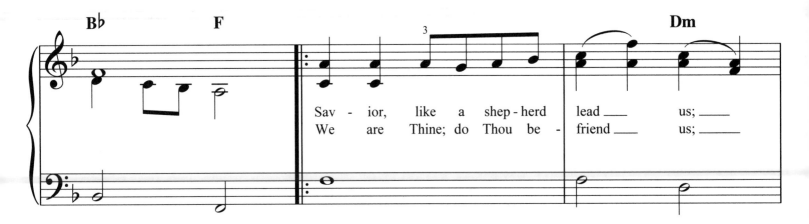

Sav - ior, like a shep - herd lead ____ us; ____
We are Thine; do Thou be - friend ____ us; ____

much we need Thy ten - der care; in Thy pleas - ant pas - tures
be the Guard - ian of our way; keep Thy flock, from sin de -

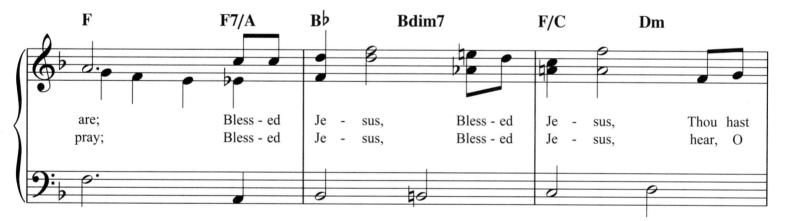

THIS IS MY FATHER'S WORLD

Words by MALTBIE D. BABCOCK
Music by FRANKLIN L. SHEPPARD

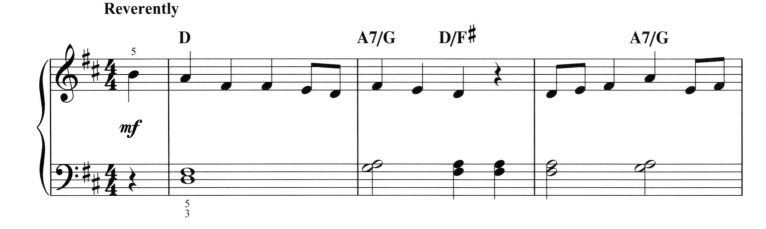

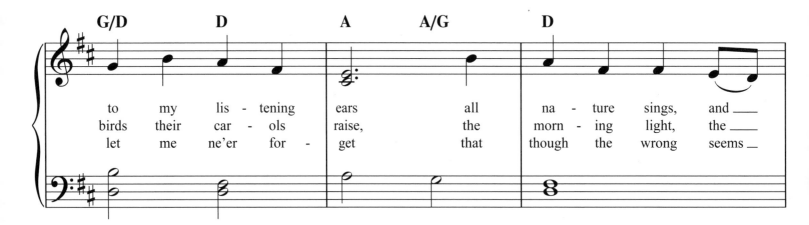

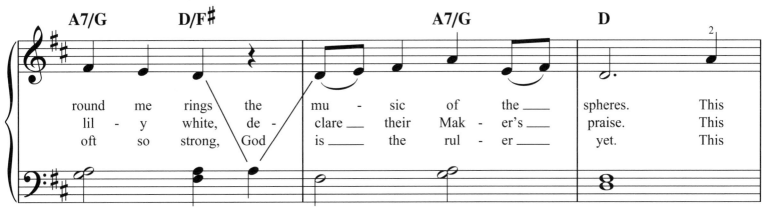

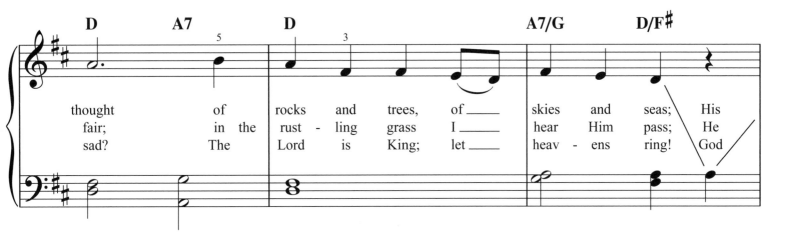

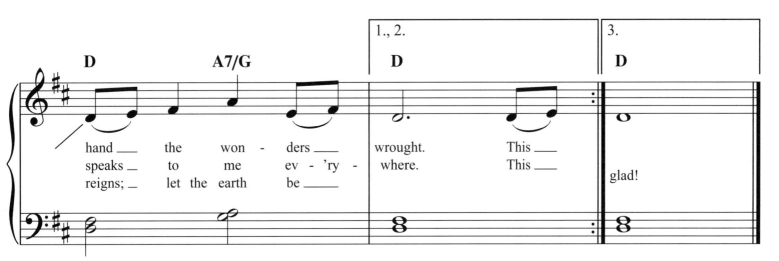

'TIS SO SWEET TO TRUST IN JESUS

Words by LOUISA M.R. STEAD
Music by WILLIAM J. KIRKPATRICK

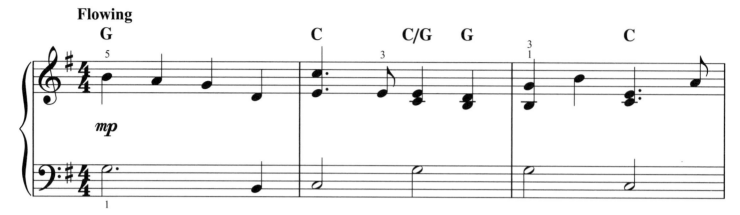

'Tis so sweet to trust in Je - sus,
O how sweet to trust in Je - sus,

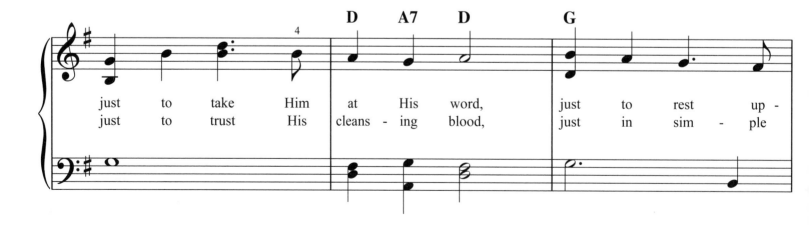

just to take Him at His word, just to rest up - le
just to trust His cleans - ing blood, just in sim - ple

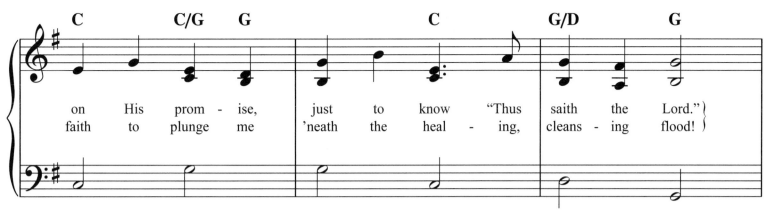

on His prom - ise, just to know "Thus saith the Lord."
faith to plunge me 'neath the heal - ing, cleans - ing flood!

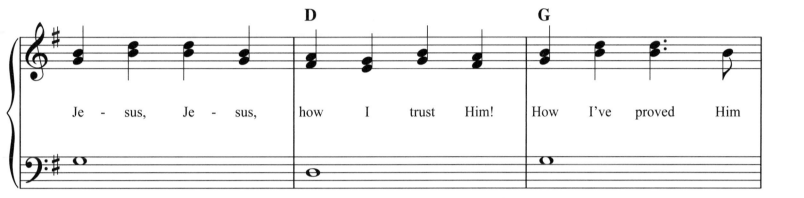

Je - sus, Je - sus, how I trust Him! How I've proved Him

o'er and o'er! Je - sus, Je - sus, pre - cious Je - sus!

O for grace to trust Him more! trust Him more!

WE GATHER TOGETHER

Words from *Nederlandtsch Gedenckclanck*
Translated by THEODORE BAKER
Netherlands Folk Melody
Arranged by EDWARD KREMSER

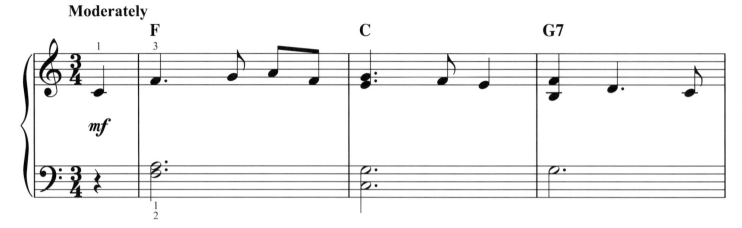

We
gath - er to - geth - er to
side us to guide us, to our
all do ex - tol Thee, Thou

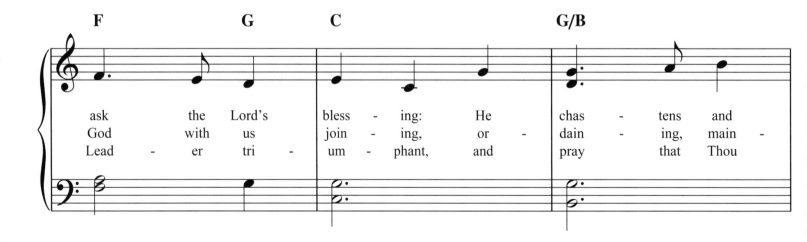

ask the Lord's bless - ing: He chas - tens and
God with us join - ing, or - dain - ing, main -
Lead - er tri - um - phant, and pray that Thou

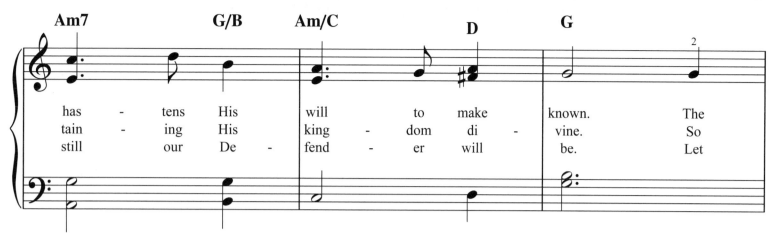

has - tens His | will to make | known. The
tain - ing His | king - dom di - | vine. So
still our De - | fend - er will | be. Let

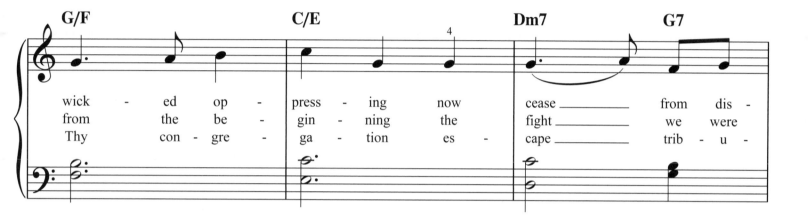

wick - ed op - | press - ing now | cease _____ from dis -
from the be - | gin - ning now the | fight _____ we were
Thy con - gre - | ga - tion es - | cape _____ trib - u -

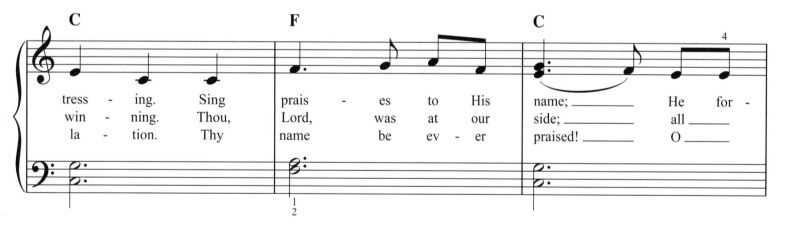

tress - ing. Sing | prais - es to His | name; _____ He for -
win - ning. Sing Thou, | Lord, was at our | side; _____ all _____
la - tion. Thy | name be ev - er | praised! _____ O _____

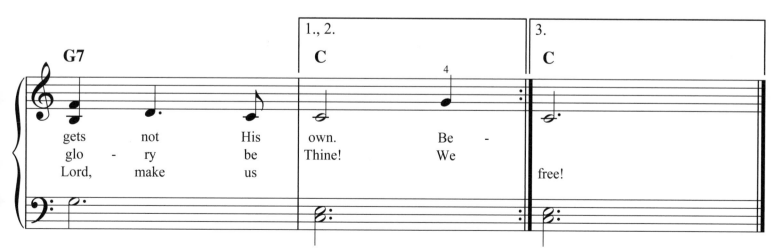

gets not His | own. Be -
glo - ry be | Thine! We
Lord, make us | free!

WERE YOU THERE?

Traditional Spiritual
Harmony by CHARLES WINFRED DOUGLAS

Moderately, with expression

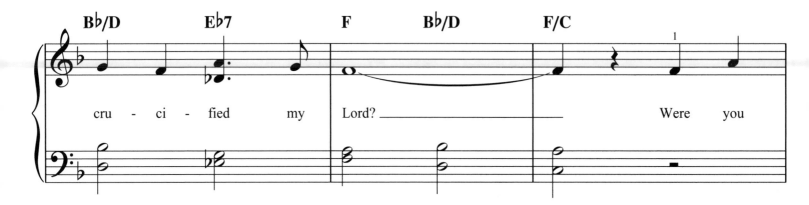

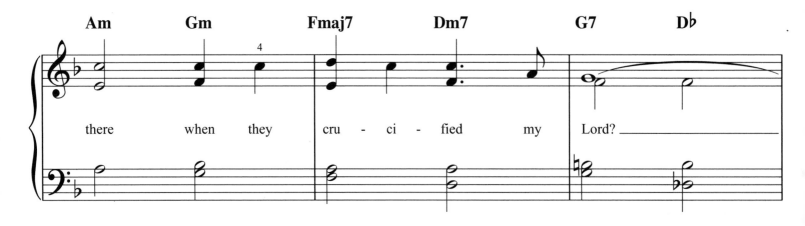

89

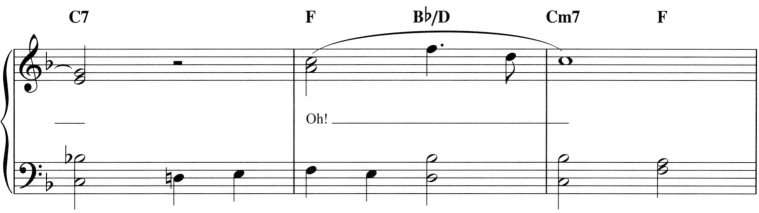

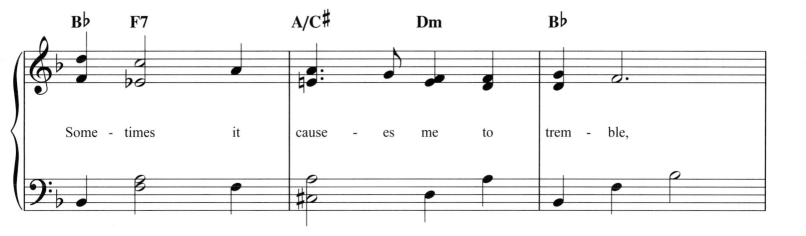

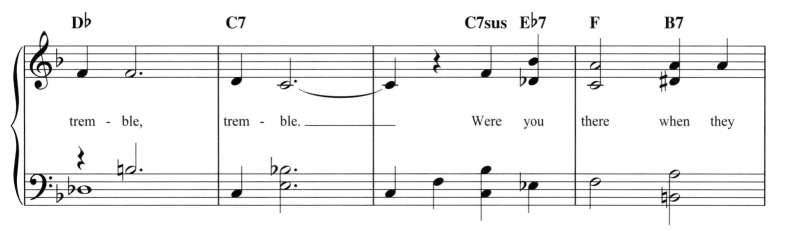

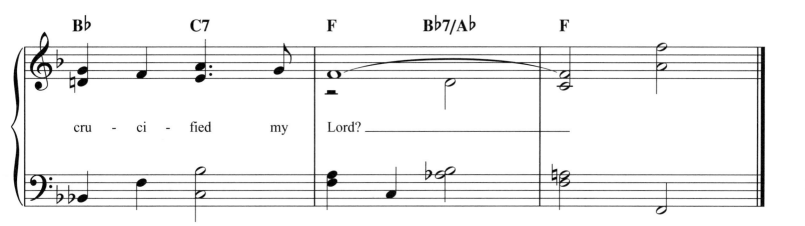

WHAT A FRIEND WE HAVE IN JESUS

Words by JOSEPH M. SCRIVEN
Music by CHARLES C. CONVERSE

What a friend we have in
Have we tri - als and temp -
Are we weak and heav - y -

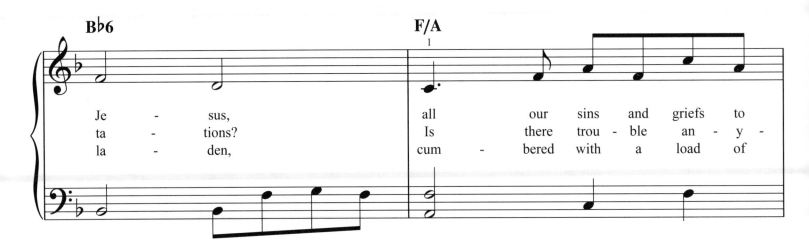

Je - sus,
ta - tions?
la - den,

all our sins and griefs to
Is there trou - ble an - y -
cum - bered with a load of

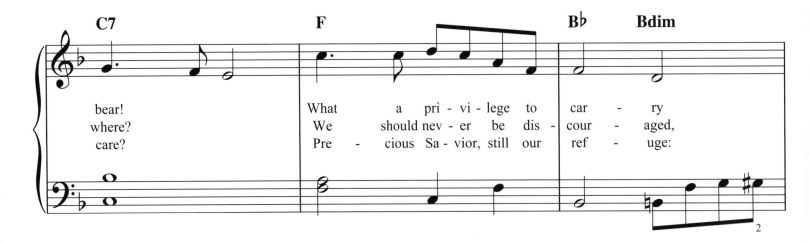

bear!
where?
care?

What a pri - vi - lege to car - ry
We should nev - er be dis - cour - aged,
Pre - cious Sa - vior, still our ref - uge:

ev - 'ry - thing to God in prayer! Oh, what peace we of - ten
take it to the Lord in prayer! Can we find a friend so
take it to the Lord in prayer. Do thy friends de - spise, for -

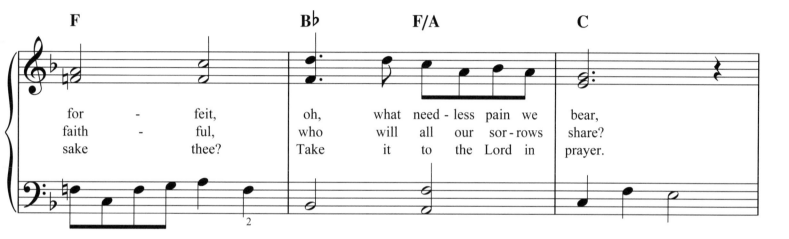

for - feit, oh, what need - less pain we bear,
faith - ful, who will all our sor - rows share?
sake thee? Take it to the Lord in prayer.

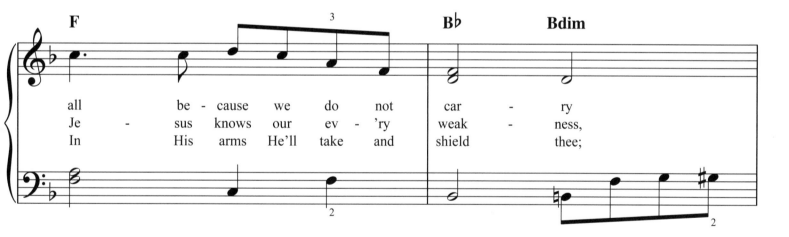

all be - cause we do not car - ry
Je - sus knows our ev - 'ry weak - ness,
In His arms He'll take and shield thee;

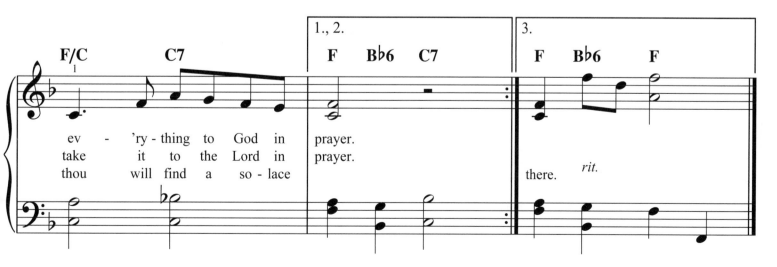

ev - 'ry - thing to God in prayer.
take it to the Lord in prayer.
thou will find a so - lace there.

WHITER THAN SNOW

Words by JAMES L. NICHOLSON
Music by WILLIAM G. FISCHER

Moderately

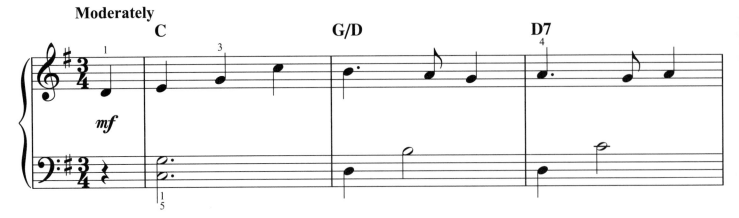

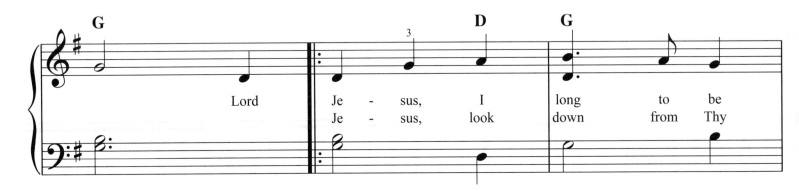

Lord Je - sus, I long to be
Je - sus, I look down from Thy

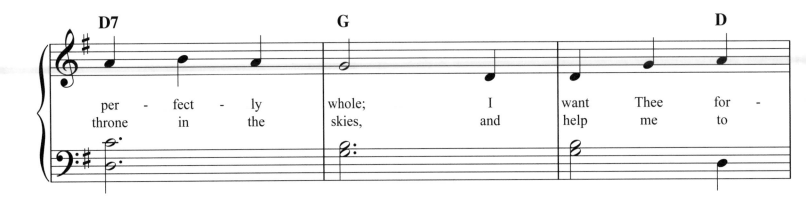

per - fect - ly whole; I want Thee for
throne in the skies, and help me to

ev - er to live in my soul, break down ev - 'ry
make a com - plete sac - ri - fice; I give up my -

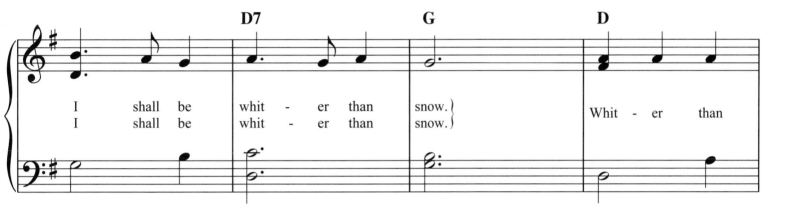

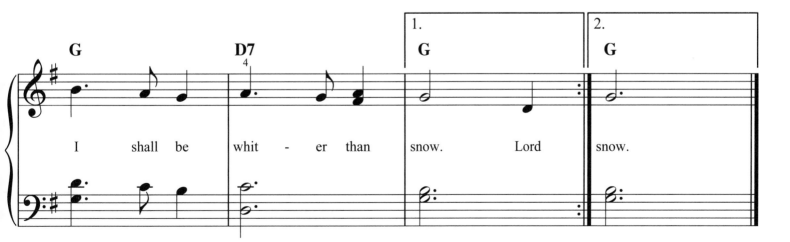

WONDROUS LOVE

Southern American Folk Hymn

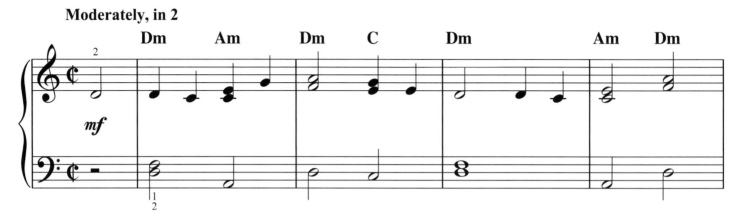

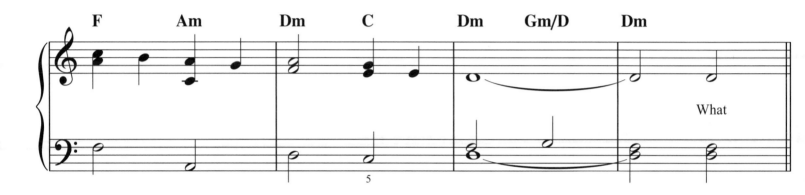

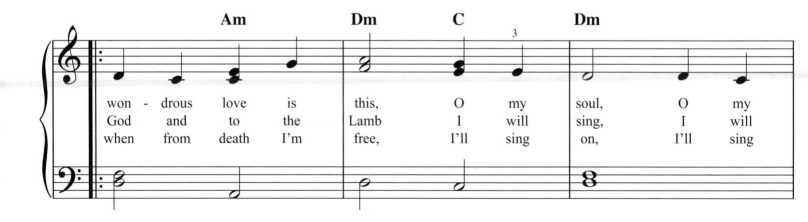

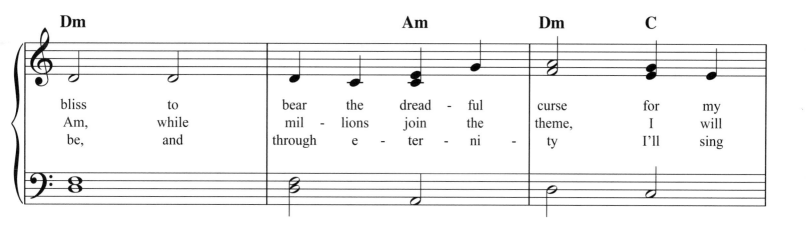

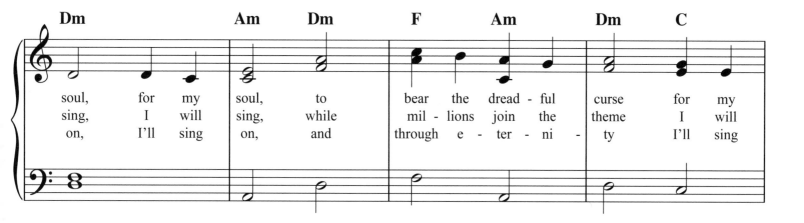

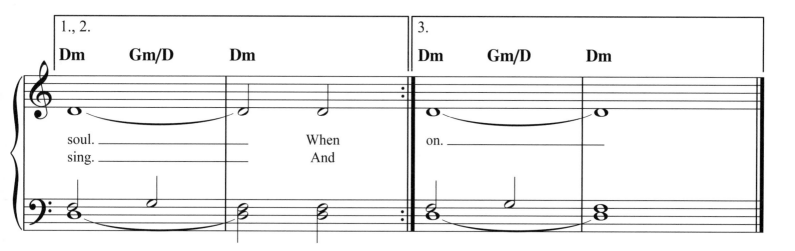

WHEN I SURVEY
THE WONDROUS CROSS

Words by ISAAC WATTS
Music arranged by LOWELL MASON
Based on Plainsong

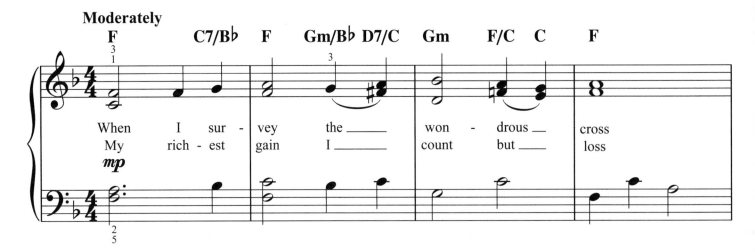

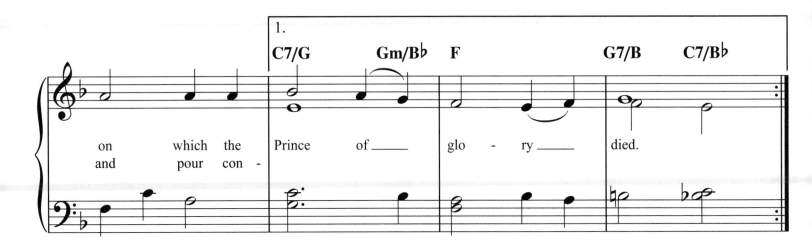

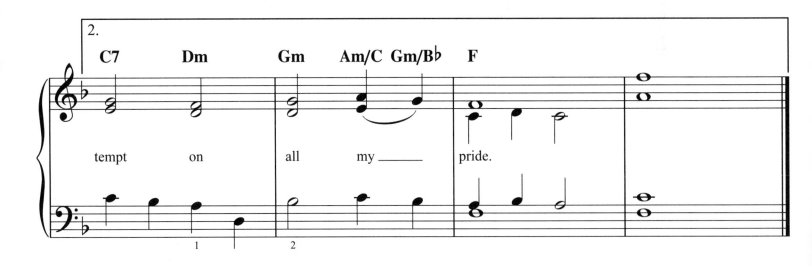